I'm Rich Beyond My Wildest Dreams

Seed money in return:
"I have recieved 10 fold in return"

RichDreams Publishing

RichDreams Publishing
4023 Birch Street, Ste A, PMB 271
Newport Beach, CA 92660-2231

Editor: Margaret Loring
Design and Layout: George Capielo
Original Painting (cover): Michael Pattinson

Visit our Web site
http://www.richdreams.com

For help email:
dear_marilyn@richdreams.com

For information on special quantity discounts for bulk purchases for
sales promotions, premiums, fund-raising or educational use contact
Promotions, RichDreams Publishing, 4023 Birch Street, Ste A, PMB
271, Newport Beach, CA 92660-2231.

I'm Rich Beyond My Wildest Dreams

"I am. I am. I am."

How to Get Everything You Want in Life

By

Thomas L. Pauley

and

Penelope J. Pauley

Published by:
RichDreams Publishing,
4023 Birch Street, Ste A, PMB 271
Newport Beach, CA 92660-2231
714-963-7757; Fax: 714-963-7762
http://www.richdreams.com

Library of Congress Cataloguing in Publication Data

ISBN – 1-929177-00-3

First Printing RichDreams Publishing October 1999
Printed in the United States of America.

Dedication

*We consider this book a gift from God.
Writing it would have been impossible without
all the help and inspiration the Universe sent
our way. We in turn wish to dedicate it to the
Good work of the world.*

Acknowledgement

We thank God and all those who do His bidding for giving us the opportunity to know this information and to write this book. We also want to thank our family and friends for their support and encouragement.

In addition, we would like to thank a few people specifically. Thank you Diane and Chris for your strength and for keeping us grounded. Thank you Margaret for your encouragement and for keeping us clear and straight. Thank you George for a keen eye and a good look. Thank you Alex and Heather for your enthusiasm and confidence. Thank you Mr. G. for the basic skills. Thank you General for the guidance and strong backbone. Thank you Dave, James, Barbara and Jill for your love, support and insight. Thank you Doug for the timely advice.

Most of all, thank you Marilyn for everything.

It is a beautiful day. The sun is warm. The sky is clear.
The band is playing a glorious tune. And you are invited
to sing along.

I'm Rich Beyond

My Wildest Dreams

I am. I am. I am.

Table of Contents

Preface

The Big Secret

Yes, there is a big secret to getting everything you want in life. It's simple. You've undoubtedly heard it before. And you probably take it for granted. It isn't the whole story, but it is essential to creating a rich, happy and healthy life. It is a Universal Law. Which means it is invested with a power and might that can take you anywhere you want to go.

Ask and you shall receive.

Humankind has known this law for thousands of years. Yet strangely enough only a small percentage of the population has ever learned how to use it in their personal and professional lives. How often have you wanted more from life, but not known how to get it? Well, now you can have everything you want. We'll show you how.

You can live the life you dream.

In this book we show you exactly how to ask, so that you may receive everything. We show you how to get the things you want in your life. And how to eliminate the things you do not want. This book will show you how you, too, can get Rich Beyond Your Wildest Dreams.

Introduction

How Rich is Rich?

At this writing I drive a big, beautiful, black Mercedes Benz S-Class. It had only 55,000 miles when I bought it. It was in perfect condition, including the golden leather upholstery. I paid $12,000 less than book value. My wife drives a very sharp Volvo station wagon in excellent condition, white with gold leather upholstery. I bought it for nothing down and $5,000 below book value. My three children each drive great cars, all of which we have purchased in the past two years. (Two new VW Jettas, and a brand new VW Golf.)

I live in a two story, five bedroom, three bath executive home with a swimming pool and hot tub. We are less than five minutes from one of the finest beaches in the world. We have all new furniture, new carpets, new pots and pans (the mirror finish kind that drives the cleaning lady nuts), new china, new flatware and plenty of new clothes to fit our new slim trim bodies.

We are healthier and happier than we have ever been. I have money in the bank. I weigh twenty pounds less than I did three months ago. If I want something, I get it. I have a Gold card with a major credit limit. We travel frequently. We eat out all the time. Every weekend we go shopping for some new thing that will enrich our lives.

My spiritual life is at an all-time high. I give more every month to spiritual works than I used to give in a couple of years. I feel good about myself and my fellow humans. I have stopped yelling at other drivers (well, most of the time). And I am even learning to love my enemies. Best of all, according to my wife, I seldom snore anymore.

My wife and I have been married for 31 years last July. We have gone through a great deal together, as have our children. Yes, we consider ourselves rich. But then so do those who used to think of us as their poor friends.

It is hard even for me to believe that less than six years ago I declared bankruptcy for the second time. My family was evicted from our home. The four drivers in our family shared two junkie cars, neither of which could be trusted to make it to the post office and back on a regular basis. But now, I am rich.

How rich is rich? There are many people who make far more money than I do (right now). Think about Bill Gates, Steven Spielberg, Shaqille O'Neal or the guy who owns the dealership where I bought my car. They, undoubtedly, have more money and more things than I do. I am happy for them. They are doing great. I hope they get richer. I certainly intend to get richer.

Rich is not having more money.

Rich is knowing the secret to getting everything you want in life.

I am rich because I've learned the secret. The secret that was right under my nose my whole life. A secret as old as Abraham and as powerful and full of possibility as a newborn child. A secret that came to me on the wings of power and might, sent from the heavens above. A secret that made me Rich Beyond My Wildest Dreams.

NOTICE!

Official Religious Disclaimer

Oh, first I must interject my basic religious disclaimer. I believe there is only one God and that all religions come from God. That God is the beginning and the end and all that lieth between. I believe God is the unknowable essence from which all things come. The Sustainer, the Healer, the Incomparable. I believe He sent many messengers, each a new chapter in one continuous revelation of God.

I accept all religions as true. I believe Jesus Christ is the Son of God. I believe Moses is the Friend of God. I believe Mohammed is the Apostle of God. I believe that Baha'u'llah is the Glory of God. I believe in Abraham, Krishna, Buddha, Zoroaster, and the Bab. I believe that all the men and women on this earth regardless of race, nationality or creed are one big family, one people, one universal consciousness.

So, if you do not believe as I do, great! You have the right to believe whatever you want. It will not change the secrets I have for you. It will not harm, hurt or diminish the power or the effectiveness of the exercises I give you. This book is not about religion. Your relationship with your creator is your business. You can call this Omniscient, All Pervasive, Omnipresent reality whatever you want. Call it a Force, Nature, the Universe, the Great

Spirit, Creation, God-She. We're only talking semantics.

But know this of a certainty – we are not alone in this life. There is a Force out there far greater than anything we can ever comprehend. It is this Universal Force that gives us everything. It is this Creative Force that has made humankind Rich Beyond Its Wildest Dreams. And it is this Force to which we turn for our own prosperity.

If I say God and you say Yahweh, or if I say Angels and you say Spirits or Guides, who cares? Maybe we'll have coffee together in Saint Moritz and talk about it sometime. Watch the sun rise over the Alps on a clear, crisp July morning. Smell the French pastry, taste the sweet cheeses, share the good times. Until then, let's get rich together. Forget our differences and make the most of what we have.

CHAPTER 1

Hawks on the Beach

This is a remarkably short book considering the gift it holds. Yes, I will tell you the secret. You will have the opportunity to be Rich Beyond Your Wildest Dreams. But first I must set the scene. To do less would be like you giving your lover a precious stone without the setting. A loose diamond is a valuable investment, but a diamond ring is a gift you'll cherish for life.

Come with me, then, to one of Southern California's least known and most intimate beaches. It is a good walk from the car down the path cut deep into the steep cliffs that protect the narrow stretch of sand and tide pools.

It was here, only a mile from Seal Island, that my story begins. Or, at least, so I originally thought. My wife, fifteen-year-old daughter and I were spending the day with my daughter's best friend and her parents. We'd known each other for a few years, but this was kind of a first date. You know, hang at the beach, enjoy the day and find out what we have in common.

Shortly after spreading our blankets and pouring on the sunscreen, I got into a conversation with Lisa, the best friend's stepmother. Lisa was into alternative thinking, most of which seemed a little far out to me, but then she said, "Did you know that the Indians in this area believed that hawks were messengers of the Great Spirit and that if a

1

hawk landed near you it meant that God had a message for you?"

I had just finished writing a video script for a major oil company's annual dealer meeting using that very concept as a central theme. I was ready to expound on my own knowledge of Native American lore when something happened that silenced us all.

Out of nowhere a hawk soared down from the heavens, circled twice above our heads and landed right next to me.

No one said anything for the longest time. It was more than strange and the coincidence was unsettling to say the least. This hawk was within maybe ten feet of me. Way out of character. Hawks are very careful to keep a good distance from possible danger. I grew up on a farm and I have never seen a hawk land on the ground let alone within a few feet of a human. Yet, I could almost reach out and touch this one.

Finally, Lisa announced what everyone was thinking. "Well, Tom, it looks like God has a message for you."

I shook my head and negated the whole weird scene with some inane joke. The hawk stayed a while longer before taking off and disappearing back into the heavens. I was quick to make sure everyone knew I didn't really believe in superstition.

Then Bob said, "One man's superstition is another man's insight." We all laughed and Lisa added, "Good thing it was only one hawk. The Indians also believed that if the hawk brought his mate to meet you, that meant the message from God was very important."

These words had no sooner left my friend's mouth when our friendly hawk reappeared from above, circled and landed again next to me, this time with his mate.

OK, to this day I still do not know what to make of all this. I do not believe in superstition, yet two incredible coincidences are equally hard to swallow. Maybe it was pure coincidence. Maybe, it was God's way of getting my attention. I do not know. But whatever the source of this remarkable play of nature, it did get my attention. And it did set the scene for a meeting that night that would eventually change my life forever.

ich Beyond My Wildest Dreams

CHAPTER 2

Accepting Your Own Good

Strange as it may seem, one of the most difficult steps in getting Rich Beyond Your Wildest Dreams is accepting your own good. Actually allowing yourself to receive the good you are due.

Most people do not expect to receive good. You have been conditioned by your perception of the events that make up your life to believe that the other shoe is going to fall at any minute. That you are not worthy of getting what you really want. That you are destined to struggle and suffer in this life. You may pray for help. You may work your fingers to the bone. You may ask for prosperity and desire the good of this world, but in the end you are not really ready to receive the gifts God sends. You have shut yourself off from the generosity of Creation.

Your good is waiting for you now.
Please open the door and let it in.

God meant for us to be rich. In every Holy Book there are verses that attest to our wealth. Baha'u'llah said it beautifully, "I created thee rich, why dost thou bring thyself down to poverty."

Accepting your own good is essential to realizing the high estate the Universe has set for you. If you refuse the good you are offered, you are refusing God and you are denying yourself that which you desire most. Not a good idea if you want to get rich.

There is the old, old, old, (I think I heard it in high school 200 years ago) story about the man caught in the flood. Surrounded by water and sitting on his front porch, the man is approached by a rescue worker in a boat. The would-be rescuer tells the man to get in the boat because the river is still rising. The man, devoutly religious, says, "No thank you, my Lord will protect me." And the boat leaves without him.

Two hours later the man has moved to the second story of his house, since the first story is now under water. This time a Sheriff's deputy steers his boat up next to the window and tells the man to get in his boat because the river is still rising. Again the man refuses saying "No thank you, my Lord will protect me." And the deputy is forced to leave without him.

An hour later the man has moved to the roof of his house when a helicopter flies over and drops a ladder for the man. Once again the man refuses, yelling up to the pilot, "No thank you, my Lord will protect me." And the chopper leaves him to die.

The man does die and goes to heaven. There he is granted a brief conversation with God. Immediately the man says, "Dear Lord, I have been a faithful servant all my life. I have always turned to You and You alone."

God nods his agreement saying, "Yes, this is true."

"Why then," the man continues, "did you leave me to die in that terrible flood."

God shakes his head and says, "I didn't mean for you die. In fact, I sent two boats and a helicopter. What more did you want?"

Accepting our own good is the first step to prosperity. Unless you accept the good you are given, nothing can come to you. If someone offers to buy you lunch or give you free tickets to a ballgame you want to see, you must accept this gift. To refuse hurts both you and the giver. You are denied your gift. The giver is denied the bounty of giving.

What's more, if you refuse to accept someone's gift, you are refusing God. Now, this leads to the first law of prosperity, but we are getting ahead of ourselves. We need to go back to that sandy beach in sunny Southern California. There's someone I want you to meet. The person who showed me the doors to my prosperity. The person who taught me how to become Rich Beyond My Wildest Dreams.

I'm Rich Beyond My Wildest Dreams

CHAPTER 3

Enter Marilyn

After putting the hawks out of mind we, Tom, Diane, Heather, Bob, Lisa, and Brooke, spent a great day playing in the cool surf and working up a healthy appetite. We had so much fun together, notwithstanding the visit from our fine feathered friends, that we all decided to go to Bob and Lisa's and grill hamburgers.

Naturally, we were tired and a bit sunburned. (Who ever remembers to use a second coat of sunscreen?) While we were cooking Bob decided we needed to meet their neighbor, "somebody we would just love." I said, "No. I'm tired and hot and cranky and I do not want to make small talk with a sweet little ole lady from Illinois who probably thinks Harry Truman is still vice president." I did not meet new people all that well back then.

Bob smiled and said, "Marilyn's kind of psychic. You'll like her," and he called her anyway. She said she was not feeling well and could not come over. I was relieved and totally disarmed when ten minutes later the back door opened and in walked this strong vibrant woman in her sixties full of good cheer and shocking blonde hair. The instant our eyes met the hairs on the back of my neck stood straight up. The electricity in the room was so thick I could feel it crackling on my skin.

Marilyn immediately walked over behind me, grabbed my shoulders and said, "I tried not coming, then I got a message that I needed to meet you, because I think I have information for you."

I was not ready for any of this. The hawks, the message, the psychic friend's hotline, none of it. But this is California, land of fruits and nuts, so I did the politically correct thing. I smiled a lot and agreed with everybody, biding my time until I could run away.

Seriously, my first meeting with Marilyn was so strangely powerful I decided to make it my business to avoid this wonderful woman for as long as humanly possible. After years of struggling from one thing to another, I had finally developed a small commercial writing business which I called an ad agency. I wrote and created brochures, videos and sundry marketing materials for, basically, one client. This paid the bills more or less. Considerably less than more, actually. My bankruptcy was recently discharged and I did not need this kind of complication in my life.

Marilyn told me she was a Prosperity teacher and that she had helped many people get the things they wanted in life. She even told me she felt strongly that she had a special message for me (something I've never heard her say to anyone else since). When I asked what the message was she told me she'd be glad to meet with me, but I had to call for an appointment. She didn't have her calendar with her. She gave me her card.

There it was. Marilyn had my message. The hawks had prepared me to receive it. They'd been quite clear. First one, then two hawks landing practically within arm's reach. Clearly, the Universe had an important message for me. And then, like the hawks, out of nowhere comes this blonde lightning bolt telling me she's the bearer of an important message. Just for me. Who could refuse such a dramatic call to action?

Maybe I was overly cautious. I don't know. Maybe I needed more time to think. Maybe I couldn't handle the truth. Who really knows these things for sure?

I do know she told me I had to call for an appointment, which to my business ears meant she was serious about her work. I know all too well that free advice is worth exactly what you pay for it. I expect to be paid for my services. And in return I expect to pay when I receive a service. (Marilyn told me later that this was the Law of Compensation.) Since I decided there was a cost involved, I dismissed the whole thing by saying to myself, "I can't afford it right now." An expensive and painful decision as it turned out.

Still, I was attracted to Marilyn's spirit from the beginning. She was honest and straightforward and behind those blue eyes I sensed a real wisdom and an exceptional talent. I have, most of my life, worked with artists, illustrators, photographers, art directors – Marilyn had that look of confidence that comes from swimming upstream successfully for a long time.

Whatever the reason, I went home that night without my message. I told myself it was because I did not want to spend any money. But I think the truth is I was afraid. I felt Marilyn's personal power. I was prepared by our friendly hawks to receive a message, a very important message. The whole day seemed orchestrated to this finale. Yet, I turned down this gift. And I paid the price of refusing a gift from God.

Know this! I refused the gift God offered me and headed off in the wrong direction. Soon my business took what seemed like a left turn into a brick wall. Oh, if I'd only known then what I know now.

All Your Good Comes From God

Contrary to popular belief your good does not come from you or your own hard work. It does not come from your boss or your client or your spouse or the general public. It does not come from luck or gambling or even Aunt Carol's will. Your good comes from one source and one source only – God.

Do you think you can work hard enough to achieve in a lifetime what the Universe can give you in an instant? It is not possible. God is the Life Giver, the Sustainer, the Prime Mover. "He giveth sustenance in plenty to whomsoever He willeth."

God created us rich. Every religion and potent philosophy in history teaches us how to tap into that heavenly storehouse. For thousands of years we have been told, "Ask and ye shall receive. Seek and ye shall find. Knock and it shall be opened unto you." Wealth is our birthright. It is the true nature of human beings. It is our destiny. It is a divine and wonderful gift, a gift so beautiful that it comes without effort. It is a gift that comes by means over which we have no control.

This is a wealth that is good for all concerned. We must never feel guilt for receiving what God has given us. How can God give us anything that would be hurtful to others? It is not possible. God is all good. In fact, Good and God are the same word. The Universe is perfect in its design. We cannot receive from God anything but good.

All we have to do is ask and the wealth of the Universe is at our fingertips. A wealth filled with happiness and joy, with fulfillment and satisfaction. A wealth we can share without loss. A wealth in every sense of the word. And perhaps, most importantly, a wealth which comes from sources beyond our control. This is not a wealth we earn, achieve, accomplish, effect, procure, win or secure by our own doing in any way whatsoever. This wealth is truly a gift from the all-encompassing power and might of the Eternal Forces of the Universe. Moreover, it is your birthright. You do not have to believe in religion or ancient philosophies to receive this wealth. It is yours for the asking. Put away your fears. Open your heart and receive your rightful share.

I will show you how to ask. It is really quite simple. So, lean back and enjoy Getting Rich Beyond Your Wildest Dreams.

Chapter 4

Ouch!

The very next morning I went to work in the new offices I had leased the month before. Leasing the offices had been a huge step for me. Committing to a year's lease, knowing I had to make my little business grow just to survive. You can imagine how I felt when my one and only client called at 10:03 am to say he would no longer be doing any work with me. He had decided over the weekend that his marketing was costing him too much money.

I went from struggling to survive to stepping into the jaws of death in one short phone call. If I knew then what I know now, the next few months would not have been nearly so painful. I would have understood the process I was going through. I would have known what to do. But I did not know then. I had the chance to know, and I turned it down. What I chose instead was the pain of going it alone. Me and my empty offices against the world. Believe me, rugged individualism is a much overrated philosophy. My thrill of victory was scraping together enough to pay the bills one more month.

Today, I know that when God closes a door, He also opens a window. All I needed to do was look for the open window, but I did not know that then. Then, I panicked.

I wasted two precious weeks pretending nothing happened. Then, after my wife threatened me with a fate worse than death, I called an old friend for a job. I worked for John when I first came to California and since then, whenever I needed a job, he was there for me. John took me in on the spot and got me back on track feeling like a salesman again. As it turned out, I only worked for him for a month, but I sure needed his help. Thank you, John.

I sometimes wonder what would have happened if I had accepted my message that August evening when I first met Marilyn. Of course, I'll never know. Once lost, a moment is gone forever. What I do know is a few months later I had accepted a position selling advertising in a fledgling Internet business. It was a business full of potential, as so many are. I, however, got paid on commissions only. No salary. No draw. I even had to pay my own office expenses, including considerable phone bills.

That is when my wife, God bless her soul, went to a baby shower for Lisa at Marilyn's house. Diane came back with a message from Marilyn: "Tell Tom he needs to come and see me. I can triple his commissions."

Triple my commissions!!! Oh, how that woman talks.

CHAPTER 5

Welcome to Marilyn's Place

It was mid-January before I finally had the nerve to call Marilyn. Five months after we first met and one month since Diane had gone to the shower for Lisa. I really felt foolish. What could Marilyn possibly tell me that would triple my commissions? I have been a salesman most of my life. I am good at it. (Though, until now, I never sustained a high level of income for any length of time.) I have been to more motivational seminars than I care to think about. I have read more books and listened to more tapes than anyone should. I know the best time to close is all the time. I know to think myself rich. I know to visualize myself making the sale. I know how to sell. I work hard at it. I am from Nebraska for crying out loud. All they know is hard work and football. What could Marilyn possibly tell me that I didn't already know?

Nothing. That was the first thing she said. "Now, I'm not going to tell you anything you don't already know. But when you leave here you'll know how to do it."

"Do what?" I asked.

"Get what you want," she replied. Then she asked the question I had not asked myself in a long time. "What do you want?"

"Well, I want to get rich," I said quickly.

She handed me a nickel and said, "Here, now you're

richer than you were when you came in."

I smiled and said, "I want to be really rich."

She said, "Why?"

"Well, so I can buy the things I really want."

"Oh, you want things. What things?"

"OK, I want a new car. I want a new house. I want a new refrigerator."

"Write it down," she said as she spread several 79-cent, wide-ruled, spiral notebooks on the table for me to choose from.

I took the purple one, opened it and started writing.

I want a new car. I want a new house. I want... She stopped me and said, "If you write it that way you will always WANT a new car, but you will never have one."

She went on to show me exactly how to ask for what I want. She explained why it works and I am going to share that with you shortly. First, I need to set the stage again. You really need to feel the power and the excitement I felt that day.

Yes, I could tell you the mechanics right now and you could write down everything you want. And if it doesn't work, who are you going to blame? Certainly not yourself. You'll blame me. Well, I want you to succeed. I want to give you everything you need to become Rich Beyond Your Wildest Dreams. So, bear with me. We are going to set the stage.

Imagine a beautiful spring afternoon, flowers in bloom, birds chirping, the sun shining and a warm breeze blowing. A typical January afternoon in Southern California. I parked in the circular drive and walked through a white trellis covered with jasmine and knocked on the already open front door. Marilyn called for me to come in, then asked me to leave my shoes by the front door. She said she wasn't as worried about dirt on her white carpets as she was about the energy the shoes might hold.

Inside, I was immediately struck by the peaceful loving atmosphere. A ficus tree by the front door was strung with white Christmas lights. A large piece of polished rose quartz sat on the kitchen bar. A large display cabinet held knick-knacks and many beautiful rocks. I even saw a couple of stuffed animals and several dolphin figurines. Nearby sat a candy bar with her great-grandson's name printed on the wrapper.

I had entered a sanctuary. I could not imagine an angry word ever uttered within these walls. I felt safe and protected, relaxed and comfortable. A far cry from the hustle and bustle of my life. No children lived here, yet there was a youthful energy that permeated my whole being. A strong, powerful force that told me Marilyn was a person of action. Someone I would respect. Someone I would trust. I have known some powerful people in my life, but this little lady from Chicago takes the cake. I am and will always be proud to know her. She never speaks unkindly of anyone. She only talks about positive things. She does not harbor prejudice or malice against anyone or any group. She is no religion and she is all religions.

Now, I'll teach you what she taught me. The secrets that will make you Rich Beyond Your Wildest Dreams.

I'm Rich Beyond My Wildest Dreams

Never, Never, Never Ask for Money

Most of my life I thought I would be rich–someday. Someday I would have millions of dollars. Someday I would have a vault full of money just like Scrooge McDuck. I would count it and swim in it and, well ... someday never came. It always seemed so easy in my imagination. In an age when the average professional basketball player makes 2.5 million dollars a year I always thought a smart guy like me could scrounge up a measly million dollars here and there. Maybe win a Lotto or two. It can't be that hard. Somebody has to win, why not me? Yet, year after year I struggled to make a living. If I had only known then what I am going to tell you now.

Never, Never, Never Ask for Money.

My number one mistake was asking for money. Big mistake. Huge. Money is too vague a concept. It means nothing to God. Money only holds the significance we give it. Since there is no universal money, it means something different to everyone. The Universe cannot supply anything as inexact as money.

You could, for example, ask for a truckload of money and end up with a truckload of those pens that are filled with chopped-up old 100 dollar bills. Probably not what you had in mind. But since there is no universal means of exchange, no universal money, who knows what you will get. Are you asking for marks, yen, dollars, pesos? Do you want this money to be counterfeit? Do you want marked bills from a bank robbery? Do you want play money from a board game? Exactly what kind of money are you asking for?

You can ask for gold, because gold is a mineral; it is something real. It can be made into jewelry, teeth, ignition points on a Rolls Royce or even coins of exchange. It is something intrinsic in itself.

God wants us to have a beautiful safe home, a strong reliable car, success in business, gold and gems, a caring love relationship, a happy family. Ask for those things and the Universe will provide them for you. Ask for money and you befuddle your request. God has absolutely no need for money, so you have absolutely no need to ask for it.

Let's say you ask for a car. Someone could leave you the exact car you want in their will. This requires no money. It only requires that you accept the bequest. You could win a car in a contest. No money needed. I have seen contests where you could win your dream house. You get the property free and clear. No money needed.

God is your provider. All your good comes from God and He does not need money. So, never, never, never ask for money.

If you want a car, a house, a new dress, a fancy leaded glass lamp, someone to love, a steady income (this is not money, it is a means of support), a family, a new pair of shoes – no matter what you want, you may have it. God will provide.

Ask the Creator to create, then get out of the way!

The first step in getting rich is to know what you want. If you do not know what you want, you had better figure it out. Because if you do not know what you want, that is exactly what you will get – nothing.

Ask specifically for what you want. God will provide it by the means He sees best. These are means over which we have no control and it may indeed involve dollars or pesos or yen. The important thing to remember is that the means are not your business nor are they under your control. They are God's means; He is doing the creating.

Many years ago I went bankrupt in the real estate business in Houston, Texas. I lost several properties. I lost my self-confidence, I lost my self-respect and, eventually, left my home to live with my wife's sister and her husband in a small house in southeastern New Mexico.

My family of five showed up on their doorstep with a thousand dollars we had garnered from selling twelve years of accumulated goods. Sold everything– the king-size bed, the couches, the Queen Anne chairs, the toaster oven, even my collection of prized Beatles albums. I had no job and, together, we had eight mouths to feed. I soon learned about God's providing for us by means over which we have no control.

The week before we arrived, Cindy, my beautiful and creative sister-in-law, gave a one-dollar donation to a 4H group at the County Fair. The 4H girl filled out a raffle ticket for Cindy's gift. Cindy doesn't believe in gambling of any kind and was in a bit of a dilemma when she won a side of beef. The girl said that if she didn't take the food someone else would get it, because they had to give the beef away. Cindy took the meat and our combined family ate well during our two-month stay.

If you want to be rich, forget the money and go for the power. The power to draw to you what you want when you want it. The secret to this power was waiting for me at Marilyn's house that January morning. Come with me and learn the secret to getting Rich Beyond Your Wildest Dreams.

CHAPTER 6

Prepare Yourself

As I slipped off my shoes and fell into the comfort and security of Marilyn's home I found myself strangely transformed. My defenses relaxed. I knew instantly that I had nothing to fear in her home. No bill collector would call. No one would reject me. I was safe. I was totally and completely protected, even without my shoes.

I have learned a great deal from Marilyn. None of it, of course, was anything I did not already know. Truth is eternal. And many have tapped into its beauty and power. It's in our music and our literature. It's in the teachings of the founders of the world's religions. It is everywhere. It permeates our very existence. On some level we all know the truth. Once you hear it, a bell rings and you know. You know the truth. You have known it forever.

Now, it is my turn to teach. I will unfold for you these same secrets to creating wealth that Marilyn taught me. Please remember, you did not hear this from me first.

You are about to begin a journey. Let us go then, you and I, to a special place in the forest of our minds, where you are safe and relaxed. Open and ready to join a very elite club of extremely wealthy people. Take a deep breath, close your eyes and take a moment to prepare yourself.

Atmosphere is very important. If you are reading this with kids yelling or at work when you are pressured to do other things like look busy – wait. Wait until you are in a quiet and receptive state. The Universe will give you all the time you need.

OK, first we are going to talk about the power of your mind. You have no clue how powerful you are. None whatsoever. And whatever power you do attribute to your mind is probably wrong. At least it was for me. I was convinced that I could do anything I set my mind to. Now, I know I do nothing and yet I get everything. Marilyn mentioned this concept to me early on, as I offer it to you. I thought she was really out there. I mean, what happened to putting your nose to the grindstone? Earning your living by the sweat of your brow? I mention this idea only to prepare you for the subtle and powerful effect you are about to create with your mind.

The power of thought is actually beyond our imagination. Yes, we know that everything humans have ever created began with a thought. But it goes beyond that. Way beyond that. We actually create our own reality.

Imagine your mind having a direct connection to the Ultimate Force of the Universe. The Ancient, All-powerful Creative Force that created the Big Bang, that built the chemical package that exploded and formed the stars, the galaxies – life as we know it. Somebody or something did this, right? Or we are part of the most incredible accident. And since there are no accidents…. OK, your mind is connected by an invisible, two-way radio channel directly to this Force. You place an order and the Force fills that order. Imagine, then, the power of your mind.

We see examples of this power all around us, but we usually choose to ignore it. Have you ever thought about calling someone and the next thing you know the phone rings and that person has called you? Have you ever known what someone was going to say before they said it? Have you ever seen someone and known instantly he or she was the person of your dreams? Love at first sight. Have you ever been drawn or attracted to a new idea or a business concept for no earthly reason other than it really interested you? Many have experienced this connection to the Guiding Force of the Universe. In fact, this is often the reason wealthy people give for their success. They "feel" guided by a sense of intuition, a hunch, an invisible connection. Once you start actualizing these secrets you too will share this experience.

I sell advertising on a large Web site. It is the nature of my job to call very busy people and present to them the opportunity we have. Well, these people get 30 to 60 phone messages a day from folks just like me. No one can return all those messages and get any work done. So, they usually do not answer the phone. When I call I get voice mail. I have called people three times a week for over a year before I got through to them. It is frustrating.

Now, using this system, things have changed. I seldom call people more than a few times until I get through. I cannot tell you how often I have been engrossed in some activity at work when I get the clear message that I should call a specific prospect. At first I wrote down the name, so that I would be sure and call later when I had finished what I was doing. That met with no real success. What did meet with incredible success was to call that person the moment I had the inspiration. Over and over again I would connect with my prospect. He or she would answer the phone and I would have a chance to either sell or close. I have heard the same comment over and over again. "I don't usually answer

27

the phone, but for some reason I picked up and I'm glad I did."

That is the power of the mind. The creative power of the mind is endless. And the creative power of your mind can barely wait to give you all that you desire.

I must tell you how I got my Mercedes. This story further reinforces both the power of the mind and the way the system works.

I wrote down that I wanted a Mercedes. I originally got a Volkswagen Jetta instead, which I always thought of as my "little Mercedes." It was a stepping stone to the Mercedes I continued to want, an S class with leather seats and a big V-8. So I wrote it down again. And again. And again. A whole year passed since I had purchased the Jetta. I had not yet seen a Mercedes appear in my driveway, and I decided to look into getting a cheaper loan rate on the VW.

I went to my bank and asked about the possibility of refinancing my Jetta. My original loan was with the automobile finance company. The girl behind the desk asked a series of questions which, as I answered, she entered into a computer. She finally told me that if the loan went through I would save $24.03 a month, but the loan would go a year longer. I said no thanks and left. About a week later I received a letter at the office informing me that I had been turned down for a loan on my 1996 Volkswagen Jetta.

Not only did I have no idea she was filling out an application, but they turned me down. I tried to ignore it. But my own bank turned me down. How could they do this to me? Didn't I put all my money in their institution for them to make a profit on? Hey, it wasn't even a bank; it was a credit union. Weren't they supposed to help the members? Over the course of a month I developed a full head of steam.

I called the president of our branch who told me to

call the man in charge of credit for the entire system. I did. He checked the application and said they were wrong; he would refinance the VW. I said, "I don't want to refinance the VW." He said, "What do you want?" Without thinking I said, "I want a loan on a new Mercedes." He thought for a minute and said, "OK." We settled on an amount and that was it. Noon the next day my daughter and I went shopping. Within two hours we found exactly the car I wanted. It was on a BMW lot and had been there for two months. They were cutting the price to move it. Standard operating procedure. We made the deal and within 24 hours of the phone call to my bank I had my Mercedes.

Everyone at the BMW dealership (including those who did not get a commission) said that my car was the cleanest used car they had ever had. That many people came in and fell in love with the car, but no one purchased it. They couldn't. It was my car. I had asked for that very car. I even created the financing up front. This was the easiest car deal I have ever made. All because of the power of the mind.

Marilyn refers to this connection between your mind and the Creative Forces of the Universe as the Subconscious Mind. Whatever you order, the Subconscious creates. And herein lies the rub – whatever you think, you order.

That means that if you think poor thoughts, you will create poverty. If you think you will not have enough money to pay the bills, then you will not have enough money to pay the bills. If you worry about losing your job, you are as good as unemployed. If you say, "We are not going to have enough money to take a vacation, enjoy a great Christmas, buy that house or pay that car payment," guess what? You are going to get exactly what you ask for

29

– not enough. This is called living in lack.

On the other hand if you think rich thoughts, you will produce wealth. If you say all my bills are paid, they are. If you say I have a new car, a house, someone to share my life with, you do. If you think kindly of other people, if you think of strangers as friends and family, your life will be rich with love. If you love living today, if you treat your work as worship, you will grow and prosper. If you think about the goodness you want and believe you have it today, you will indeed become Rich Beyond Your Wildest Dreams.

THE THIRD LAW OF PROSPERITY

The Universal Law of Cause and Effect

What goes around comes around. Every action has an opposite reaction. People who live in glass houses should not throw stones. You have heard about the law of Cause and Effect all your life. You know it's true. What you put out comes back to haunt you or help you. What you may not have understood is how this law combines with the Law of Multiplication to dramatically impact your success.

Please note the following diagram. I see it in my sleep. For over two years practically every time I asked Marilyn a question she drew this diagram. Memorize it, because it is one of the keys to your success.

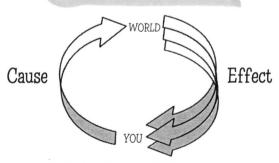

Whatever you put out into the world,
you get back multiplied.

Cause ⟶ WORLD ⟶ Effect ⟶ YOU

Marilyn's *Cause and Effect* Diagram

31

You will undoubtedly notice that there is one line going out to others and many lines coming back to you. This is the Law of Multiplication. What you put out gets multiplied at least tenfold. If you put out positive energy, you get back a multitude of good. If you put out negative energy, you get that back multiplied also. If you put out anger, you get back a storm of anger. If you put out happiness, you get back a storehouse of happiness.

Very simply this means every time you say, write or think mean-spirited, ugly, hurtful or hateful things about anyone for any reason, you are putting out negative energy. You are creating for yourself exactly what you have ordered for others. Only you get it ten, fifteen, maybe twenty times worse. You are never really angry at anyone else. You are only talking about yourself.

A friend of mine who is normally in excellent health called one afternoon in the grip of great pain and suffering. She felt that she had very little reason to live anymore, that her life was horrible. She said that her son had fallen from his motor scooter and broken his collarbone. Her mate and she were fighting constantly. Her cat had marked her bedroom for the third time that week. She was too sick to go to work but she needed the money because her daughter's college tuition was due, a bill which was rightfully the obligation of her ex-husband. The Blankety-blank-blank-blank. Finally, we got to the source of the problem.

She was furious at her ex-husband and had been for a long time. She was thinking and speaking of him in less than complementary terms. She was creating an order for incredible pain and suffering for HERSELF!

Once she recognized that she was creating her own misfortune and disease, she changed her attitude and her life brightened immediately. She decided that her ex was doing the best he could. She decided it was her responsibility to deal with him in the best way she could. She decided to expect nothing from him and always work through her lawyer when it involved the kids. She protected herself by giving goodness out to the world.

Now, in this example, negative energy returns quickly to the sender. In other cases it can take years before that pain comes back to you. The only thing you can be sure of is that it will come back.

The opposite is also true. If you send out loving, kind, magnanimous and caring words, thoughts and deeds, you will receive that goodness back multiplied. What you give is what you get. No doubt about it.

Sending out negative energy is a bad habit. This is something we all have to work on every day. It is entirely too easy to get angry at other drivers, neighbors, bosses, friends or loved ones. It is too easy to call them names. Horrible names you really do not mean. It is entirely too easy to think poorly of someone because of their economic, racial, religious or ethnic background. It is too easy to hate people because they are different. It is too easy to let differences override similarities, to shun and deride that which is outside of that with which you are comfortable. And what good does it do? You are only talking about yourself. It only hurts you. You are simply setting yourself up for a big negative payback. Besides we are not here to judge. We are here to get rich.

Change your attitudes. Develop new habits. Think good thoughts. You can do this. I did. Every time you say something negative about yourself or anyone else, stop and forgive yourself, then correct your thinking. Allow only good and kind thoughts to enter your mind or leave your mouth. Imagine yourself sowing golden seeds of love and kindness everywhere you go. The result is a harvest Rich Beyond Your Wildest Dreams.

ATTENTION!

Do not turn this page until you are prepared.

You must have a 79-cent wide-ruled, spiral note-book to continue. If you do not have one, stop right now and go get one. Writing in the notebook is a vital part of using this system of obtaining wealth. You cannot do this work without a 79-cent wide-ruled, spiral notebook. Do not try. Do not read on thinking you will do it later. Stop and go get a 79-cent wide-ruled, spiral notebook.

Now, make sure you have the privacy and time, at least an hour, to complete the next chapter. It is better that you are not disturbed by friends, family, co-workers, or pressing engagements while you do your work. Learning is work and you are learning a new system. As simple as all this may seem you need quiet space and privacy to continue. It's up to you, but as my father used to say, "A job worth doing is worth doing right."

I'm Rich Beyond My Wildest Dreams

CHAPTER 7

What Do You Want?

Do you want a new car? Do you want a new house? Do you want a new job? Do you want a loving, caring relationship? Do you want to live your life in lack? Or do you want to live your life Rich Beyond Your Wildest Dreams? Whatever you want you can have.

It is just as easy to live rich as it is to live poor. The difference is you. All you have to do is decide what you want and you can have it. I am about to tell you how. Are you in a quiet place? Are you in a private, secure place? Can you give this project an hour of your time without interruption? If your answers are yes, let's get started. You are about to take the first step to a prosperous new life. Start by taking out your 79-cent wide-ruled, spiral notebook.

Open your notebook to the inside cover and in big letters write the following:

All this by Divine Right, Divine Inspiration, Divine Intervention, Divine Timing and with Good for all concerned.

The reason you write that statement is to cover your backside. You may desire something that God does not desire for you. You ask for the things you prefer to have and the Universe decides. The bottom line is if you are supposed to have something, you'll get it. If not, you wouldn't want it anyway.

Important! Skip the first page. You will write something here later. Turn to the second page of your notebook. Write on only one side of a page. Skip every other line. The reason you write on only one side of a page is to make use of the Law of Abundance, which says you have an unlimited supply, inexhaustible resources. There is more than enough paper. By not skipping lines and using both sides of the page you are reflecting someone who has money problems or meager resources. Is this what you what? Of course not. You are rich. You have at your fingertips all the resources you could ever use. Expand your thinking; write on one side of the page only.

Page two is actually the second sheet of paper. On the top of this second sheet of paper write *My List.*

Now, make a list. Write down a list of everything you want as though you already have it. Use the present tense or the past tense. I have a new car. I had a wonderful evening at the opera. I have a loving, caring, romantic relationship. It does not matter if you have done something like this before. Make the list. Do it exactly as shown. This is an important part of this system for creating wealth.

Be careful not to write that you *want* something or that you *will* have something. If you write, "I want a new car," your subconscious hears that you want to WANT a new car. If you say, "I will have a new car," you are saying that you may desire this sometime in the future, but not now. The Creative Force of the Universe does not hear that you want to HAVE a new car. So, tell your subconscious what it wants to hear. *I have a new car.*

In the beginning this was difficult for me. I felt like I was lying or cheating somehow. I did not have a new car, but I wanted one. Why say, *I have one?* The answer is you are creating something. Something tangible for you to use, have or experience in the present. If you create it in the future, you will never get the chance to enjoy your desire because, as we all know, tomorrow never comes. By writing down what you want in the present or past tense you are telling the Universe what you want to have in your possession at this exact point in time. The Universe then makes what you want and gives it to you in your existing time line. The Universe only understands very simple, direct descriptions. I have a big screen TV. I had a good time at the theater. I have a new chair. This will get you what you want when you want it.

Think of the words *want* and *will* as code words that tell the Universe to wait. To cancel your order. These words tell the production line to shut down and take a break. With a little experience you will feel comfortable using only the present tense and the past tense to describe your desire.

Now, we are going to start your list. I am not there with you and I do not know exactly what you want. Hopefully you do. I will assume you want certain things. I will assume you want a new car, for example. If you are absolutely opposed to having a new car, pretend. You can always tear the page out later and throw it away.

Start writing a list of what you want. Write one desire on every other line and only on one side of the paper. These notebooks are cheap. I go through several a month. Give yourself plenty of room to create. By following this system you are asking God to allow you to live in abundance. Start now. Skip lines. Write on one side only. Plenty of room. Here is an example of what a list might look like.

My List

1. I have a new car.
2. I am now living in my new home.
3. I have a new sofa.
4. I am slim, trim and healthy.
5. I love my new job.
6. I have many new friends.
7. I have season tickets to the Lakers' games.
8. I have a wonderful love relationship.
9. I have a fantastic sex life.
10. My children/parents are safe and protected.
11. My bodily organs work correctly.
12. I have an active social life.
13. I have a large, dependable, steady income.
14. I have new sheets for my bed.
15. I am on a cruise vacation to Hawaii.

This list can go on forever. Make it as long as you like. In fact, write until you feel that you have exhausted every desire you have ever had. Write down businesses you want to own. Write down the things you want to do. You should even write down the little things like *I have renewed my driver's license* or *I have returned the library books*. Write down how you want your life to be – the parameters. Always and only the parameters. Do not get too specific yet. Just write down what you want. Keep the adjectives to a minimum. We'll get into the details later. For now, paint with broad brush strokes. Draw the outline. Define the objects of your desire in the most general terms.

It is a good idea to write, *I have a beautiful new or like-new car*. This gives the Universe the opportunity to get you a really great deal. You may, for example, get a great deal on a one-month-old car. Or maybe a car that someone bought and never drove.

The first time I did this I wrote down "I have a new Mercedes Benz. It is green." I did this more as a wish than a real belief. I did not think it was possible for me to buy a new Mercedes Benz, but I really wanted an MB, so I wrote it down. What I got was new and green, and the first step to getting a big Mercedes Benz. Within six weeks I bought a brand-new green Volkswagen Jetta, right off the dealer's lot. I had been driving an old clunker with loud squeaky brakes and no muffler. To me the Jetta was a dream come true. Later, my German mechanic friend, Wolfgang, said, "Ya got da Jetta. Dis is a little Mercedes, ya?" The Universe gave me exactly what I asked for.

Breathing life into what you want begins with this simple LIST. Write down what you want. Next, VISUAL-IZE what you want. Close your eyes and in your mind see yourself possessing what you've written down. You must have a clear vision of what you want. Then, feel the joy of having what you want. Imagine what it feels like to enjoy having the things you've asked for. Get ENTHUSIASTIC about having what you want. This is extremely important. As Benjamin Franklin said, "Nothing great comes without enthusiasm." Enthusiasm is the kinetic bond that gives cohesion to your desires. Writing your list changes dreams into requests or preferences. Visualization changes your requests into solid orders, compelling desires. But it is enthusiasm that puts these desires into your heart. And it is only in your heart that the Universe looks for your orders, your desires. Do all three things and you will have what you want. In fact, this is the secret to getting anything you want. Anything. And it is not just a good idea – it is the law.

List + Visualize + Enthusiasm = Getting what you want

Start with your car. Write down exactly what you want. Close your eyes and create in your mind a clear image of what your car looks like. See your car in the color you want and from every angle. Visualize yourself behind the steering wheel. Imagine the feel and smell of the leather. See yourself driving along your favorite highway. Experience in your mind the power of acceleration and the wind in your hair. Now, feel the overwhelming joy you receive taking delivery of YOUR NEW CAR. Savor the feeling of excitement you get driving your new car home for the first time. Do what it takes to make this car real for you. Go to a dealership and test drive the car you have asked for. Get excited about this vehicle. This is your car. Love it. Want it. Own it.

Put images and enthusiasm into the rest of your list. In your mind walk through the home you want. Smell the fresh paint and new carpet. See each and every room. Look at every angle. Imagine this home filled with your prized personal possessions. Take this a step further and get pictures of the things you want inside your home. Go look at refrigerators, wallpaper or pool supplies. Do what it takes to make what you have asked for real in your mind. If it is a relationship you have asked for, cut out a picture from a magazine of a couple in a loving pose. Look at wedding rings. Try some on. Go to weddings. Whatever it is that you want – touch it, see it, feel it. Get excited about having it. Put the things you want in your heart. They are yours, all yours.

Now, let go. Detach yourself from what you want. You still want it, but you have given the Universe power over its creation and acquisition. You do not earn it. You do not have to deserve it. You do not have to accomplish, achieve or fulfill anything. Your job is to ask and wait. So, let it go. Detach. Turn your back. Let the Creator do His part. Besides you have got more paperwork to do. There are still a few details remaining for you to get Rich Beyond Your Wildest Dreams.

I'm Rich Beyond My Wildest Dreams

Please Note!

You do not have to believe any of this. Not one single word. I don't care. The Universe doesn't care. Nobody cares. You can believe all this or not. You can take what you want and disregard the rest. It is up to you entirely.

Because it doesn't matter what you believe.

Do the work described here, follow this system for gaining wealth and you will prosper. Period. The laws work regardless of what you believe.

I'm Rich Beyond My Wildest Dreams

CHAPTER 8

Detailing Your Wealth

Again, make sure you have plenty of undisturbed time available before you begin this chapter. Creating something by using your mind demands concentration and effort. You have already written the list of things you want in your life. These are really preferences. Things you would prefer to have. The Universe then decides when, how, and even if, you get them. Now, you are going to detail that list.

Once you have written the things you want, turn ahead a few pages, maybe ten or twelve. You are leaving room to add more later. At the top of that page write a subject, like *My New Car*. Then, describe in detail the car you want in the same asking style. Limit each line to one description. Skip every other line. Utilize the Law of Abundance – write on one side of the paper only. Use as many pages as necessary for every subject. Skip a page or two between subjects. You may need to add more detail later. You're rich – act like it. You are creating superlative wealth. The cost of a spiral notebook is insignificant.

Incidentally, there are specific reasons you put only one description on a line. Each line is an order. The more complex the order the more difficult it is for the Universe to fulfill all the elements at exactly the same moment. When Marilyn first started writing down her desires she wrote, "I have a new beige purse with matching beige shoes." She was working in a craft store in a small community outside of Chicago. At lunch she happened into a shoe store and found exactly the beige shoes she wanted, but no purse. She bought the shoes and hurried back to her store without getting any lunch. She had the anxious feeling she was taking too long a lunch break by looking at shoes. She no more than walked into the store when a woman came in selling purses. Yes, there was the beige purse that matched her shoes exactly. She bought the purse about five minutes after buying the shoes. See, the Universe had to deliver her entire order at one time. She had to miss lunch for that to happen and we are talking about rather easy-to-find items. What if you wanted a like-new, red, Isuzu Rodeo with the fancy interior, a 20-disk CD changer, high-performance tires and the special chrome wheels. On one line that could take a while. Put each detail on a separate line and God can deliver what you want faster and easier. Maybe you get the CD changer and the tires after you buy the car.

Also, some of the specifics you write down may not be what the Universe wants you to have. These are only preferences. You have already asked that it only be for your Highest Good. And that your requests be guided by Divine Right, Divine Inspiration, Divine Timing and Divine Intervention with Good for all concerned. Let the Universe decide which details it delivers.

Write a single description on each line. Be as specific as you want. Write as many descriptions as you want. Your list will look something like this:

My New Car

1. I have a new or like-new car.
2. My new car is black.
3. My new car has a 12-cylinder engine.
4. My car has a leather interior.
5. My car is a Mercedes-Benz.
6. My Mercedes is an S-600.
7. It has cup holders.
8. It has a CD player.
9. It has an AM/FM radio.
10. It has an excellent speaker system.
11. It has a 20-disk CD changer.
12. My car has a lumbar-adjustable driver's seat.
13. My new car has the parchment color interior.

Write down what you want exactly as I have written it. Certainly, you may change the description to suit your desires. That is the whole idea of this exercise. Make it work for you. Get what you want.

The following descriptions are very helpful and I suggest you use them. You are describing more than a car. You are describing the conditions of your life. Do you want to use your house payment money to buy this car? Of course not. You are not looking for a burden. You want a pleasant, carefree experience with your new vehicle. Describe as clearly as possible the circumstances surrounding your situation. And avoid making limitations on the Universe.

14. My new car is easily paid for.
15. My car is completely insured.
16. The insurance is easily paid for.

17. My car runs great.
18. My car has an excellent warrantee.
19. Everyone who rides in my car is safe and protected at all times.
20. Only those who are for my highest and best good may ride in my car.
21. My new car is seeking me as I am seeking it and the Law of Attraction brings us together with love and understanding.
22. I have the correct car for me.

Ask the Universe for all the good you can imagine. Protect yourself and your loved ones. The more specific you are the better. Your job is to define the parameters of what you want so God can fill the order as precisely and quickly as possible, as in the illustration below.

Define the parameters of what you want!

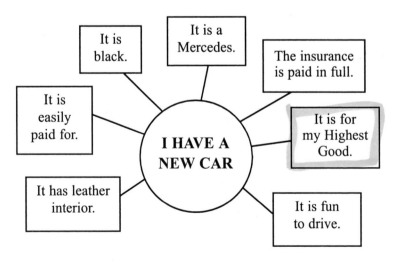

Now that you have described the car you want, turn to a new page and detail a new subject, like *My Home.* Continue detailing new subjects until you have detailed everything on your list of desires from Chapter 7. Some detail lists will be long, some will be short. As you detail you may think of new ideas for the list of desires. Go back and add them. You are detailing your own new rich life. Ask for everything you want. More is always better. Below I have included two more sample lists. Have fun. You can have whatever your mind desires. Be sure to leave room on big items like a home. You may want to go back later to add detail for things like wallpaper and fixtures.

My Home

1. I am now living in my new home.
2. I own my home.
3. It is a house.
4. It has five bedrooms.
5. It has three bathrooms.
6. It has a beautiful swimming pool.
7. The swimming pool is heated.
8. The heat for my swimming pool is easily paid for.
9. My new home is large and roomy.
10. My new home is a pleasant drive from my office.
11. My new home is fully insured.
12. Only those who are for my highest good may come into my home.
13. Everyone who is in my home is safe and protected at all times.
14. My new home is easily paid for.

15. My new home is seeking me as I am seeking it and the Law of Attraction brings us together with love and understanding.
16. It is the correct home for me.
17. My new home is mine by Divine Right.

My Couch

1. I have a beautiful new couch.
2. I have a matching love seat.
3. My new couch is light in color.
4. It has a modern, attractive design.
5. It is comfortable for me to sit on.
6. It supports my back comfortably.
7. It is easily paid for.
8. My new couch is seeking me as I am seeking it and the Law of Attraction brings us together with love and understanding.
9. It is the correct couch for me.

Recently, my oldest daughter graduated from college and moved into an apartment of her own. My wife and I decided to give her a bed. I asked my daughter to write down what she wanted. (You cannot write down what you want other people to have. This is absolutely against Spiritual Law.) She included items 8 and 9: *It is seeking me as I am seeking it...* and *It is the correct bed for me.* Here is why they are included.

Penelope and I went to every department store and bed store we could find. We found several good beds, but none that we felt compelled to buy. Now, I am not a big shopper. I will look around some, but this became a month-long search. It got so bad, I finally told her she had to decide. I was tired of shopping. In fact, I stopped caring if we ever found her bed. She agreed. So instead of more shopping one Sunday I fell asleep in front of a football game and Penelope went to her boyfriend's house.

When she got there, she read the Sunday paper and found a sale on beds at Sears. We had never considered Sears, but it was a great sale. We went the next day. We each took a turn lying on one of the beds. Neither of us had any doubt. This was THE bed. It was a better bed than we had seen previously and it was on sale for several hundred dollars less than we would have paid elsewhere.

How did we find her bed? We stopped caring if we ever found it. This is detachment. This is all about how you feel. We felt that we already had the bed, but at the same time we did not care if we had the bed.

Two things to remember here. First, since the "correct" bed was "seeking" us, we were not allowed to buy until we found the right one. Secondly, we did not find the bed until we stopped caring. This is part of detachment, which we cover in more detail later. Not until we grew tired of shopping were we detached enough for the Universe to show us where to look. What a small price to pay for getting Rich Beyond Your Wildest Dreams.

I'm Rich Beyond My Wildest Dreams

CHAPTER 9

Defining Your Relationships

What good is having a lot of stuff if you go through life alone? Even the most introverted people I know need friends. We are social and sexual beings. We need friends in whom to confide, business and intellectual associations to stimulate our minds and intimate tender relationships to soothe our souls. We need a partner to love and a family to cherish. Without these all-important relationships life can seem a little empty. So, if you are Rich Beyond Your Wildest Dreams, why not have it all? Relationships are as much a part of our success and happiness as a new car or a beautiful, safe home. You deserve to have a wealth of personal relationships. Be my guest. It certainly is your right.

No one is perfect. No matter how spiritual, clever or rich individuals may be, they are not perfect. This is an imperfect world and we are part of that world. We, too, are imperfect. We make mistakes, we grow, we learn – this is the very reason we are in this life. We are here to learn such things as patience, charity, love, kindness, understanding and tolerance. Which means we all have plenty of work to do on relationships. By writing down what you want in your relationships, you will attract and keep the kind of relationships that lead to a happy, loving, prosperous life.

We might as well start with the big one – your marriage. Detail the marriage you want. Certainly this relationship deserves a few minutes for planning. Whether you are married or single, male or female, write down a description of the marriage you want right now. Open the 79-cent notebook and write down these examples. Remember this is an exercise, so if you do not like what is written here, you can always change it. Make it apply to you. Be specific, because you just may get exactly what you ask for. At the top of the page write *My Marriage.*

My Marriage

1. We are totally compatible in every area.
2. We respect each other tremendously.
3. We are on the same wavelength about marriage.
4. We have a monogamous relationship; he is faithful to me, as I am to him.
5. It is a prosperous marriage.
6. He is financially responsible (i.e., to the family).
7. He supports me in everything I do.
8. The love between the two of us is more than I could ever have imagined.
9. He gives me gifts at the most unexpected times.
10. He gives me freedom to be me, as I do him.
11. We are great friends.
12. We are spiritually compatible.
13. Children arrive at the appropriate times – our choosing.
14. All the children are healthy.
15. We have incredible sex and enjoy each other in this capacity.
16. We are like-minded.
17. We have tons and tons of fun together.
18. We have many wonderful surprises in our marriage.

19. We take fun vacations together.
20. We have a happy family.
21. I am with the correct person for me.
22. I am married to my divine complement.
23. The marriage I am seeking is seeking me and the Law of Attraction brings us together in love and understanding.

If you are more comfortable with someone having the same cultural, racial or ethnic background as you do, then add these details to your list. That's fine. This is your life; choose what you want. Besides, these are only preferences. God has creative control.

Here's something else to think about when writing down relationships. You must at all times remain an individual. You cannot write down preferences for someone else. You cannot make your life dependent upon someone else or them upon you. Just as two trees must remain separate and distinct, you and your partner must each remain strong and firmly rooted as individuals. If one of our two trees leans too heavily upon the other, neither tree will grow properly. The same is true of people. Once you give up your individuality, you become weak. This weakness can break you, your partner, your offspring, and your marriage.

Ask only for the circumstances surrounding a relationship. Ask for an honest and faithful partner. Never ask for a specific individual to be honest and faithful. You cannot determine what others are to have or how they are to behave. That is a breach of Universal Law. It is a dangerous practice. We must each choose our own life for ourselves. This is the responsibility of every individual on the face of the earth. We do not have the right to interfere with anyone's personal growth. If you do try to control someone else, to decide what is best for them, you may be asking for more trouble than you care to have. The best idea is to concentrate on your own growth and let others take care of their lives.

You may, however, ask that you know how and where a particular individual fits into your life. You may write, *I now know how and where John fits into my life.* Here you are asking for information about your life. And you are leaving John to deal with his own life. Draw the boundaries and let the Universe fill in the details.

I need to say a word about divorce. My parents got divorced when I was nine years old. I have suffered emotional scars from their divorce. Maybe it made me a better person, I do not know. I know it took a lot of therapy to realize their divorce was not my fault. And I know I always worked a little harder to keep my own marriage together because I had seen divorce up close and personal. Naturally, I am not an advocate of divorce. I celebrated my 30th wedding anniversary in the summer of 1998 and we earned the wonderful party our kids put together.

On the other hand, some marriages are not meant to be. I know a beautiful, energetic and vivacious woman who was married to an absolutely negative individual. After one hour in their home my whole family encouraged her to get divorced. He was physically and emotionally abusive. There is no excuse for that. Even more importantly, there was no excuse for raising their two children in that relationship. He may have been doing the best he could for him, but she could do better for herself. She did get divorced and found a great job where she met a new man who treats her like a queen and loves her kids. She sent us an email the other day saying that they had just received loan approval on the house they are buying together. It is her first house and she can now have a few things she never had before, like a garden and a kitty.

Trust God to guide you in heavy matters like divorce. Ask for His aid and assistance. Ask for His guidance. You will see the truth and you will know what to do. Hopefully, you will not have to deal with this problem, but things happen. If you are not meant to be with someone, your situation could change very quickly.

Ask that you have the correct relationship for you. Not the perfect relationship. We live in an imperfect world. In fact, that is the whole point of this life – to grow toward perfection. Everybody makes mistakes. Everybody has lessons to learn. Everybody and everything in this big beautiful world is a bundle of imperfection. Trees grow crooked. Animals mutate and evolve. People are always less than perfect. To ask for the perfect relationship is to ask for the impossible. There is no such thing. We live in a bubbling stew that constantly changes. Change, not perfection, is the only constant in this life. Ask for the correct relationship; the Universe will smile on you.

If you are married or already in a serious relationship, you may want to work on this part together. Do not, however, force your significant other to join in if he or she is not interested. It is against Spiritual Law to tell someone else what to do. You are creating a unity, a oneness, a marriage that will serve as your fortress of well-being. Your union will create an existence which is greater than the combination of two individuals. Just remember to remain individuals in writing down this relationship.

Again, write the circumstances surrounding the situation. Avoid naming specific individuals. Let the Creative Forces of Life work for you. You do not have to do it all.

If you find that a relationship is over, end it loving-ly. As difficult as that sounds, always end a relationship without anger or resentment. All this means is that the Law of Attraction is lifted from you. Your relationship has served its purpose. You both have other things to learn, places to go, people to meet. Part friendly, if not friends. Anger and resentment will not help you on your journey. They are a heavy burden that will weigh you down, hinder your progress, and may even keep you from finding your correct partner.

Now that you have detailed your marriage, write down the other relationships in your life. Skip a few pages and write *My Friends* at the top of a page. Now, write down exactly what you want in relationships with your friends. Repeat this process for *My Customers, My Business Associates, My Partners, My Employers, My Vendors, My Clients, My Employees*...you get the idea.

Always ask that only those who are for your highest good be allowed in your life. Do not ask that you be for their highest good. Again this is against Spiritual Law. You are in this life to develop yourself. You are here to learn and grow. Your job is not to develop anyone else, just you. Consequently, you must be around like-minded individuals to survive. If someone you care about is very negative, you may be for their highest good, but they may not be for your highest good.

Once you ask that everyone in your life is for your highest good, things will change. People who are not for your highest good will drift away from you. Let them. You will find new friends, new relationships. You will wake up one day and discover you have a new set of friends. Friends that are closer and better for your life. Some of your old friends may stay close. Others may come back later. The Universe has a way of making life easy if you let it.

Now that you have a feeling for how to write down relationships, do yourself a huge favor. Take some time and write down the rest of your life. Define, in broad brush strokes, the circumstances surrounding the rest of your life. Describe the kind of life you want to live. Do you want to be a parent? Do you want to live in the security of a small town? Or would you feel more comfortable riding the adventure of big-time corporate America? Do you want to travel? Do you want a nanny for your children? Would you rather have a home-based business and enjoy your kids full-time? You can have whatever you want. The sooner you define your life, the easier it is for the Universe to create it for you.

Plan ahead and avoid roadblocks. You have heard this all your life. Now is your chance to do some real planning. Write down the jobs or businesses you want to have. Write down the kind of client, employee or employer relationships you want to have. It is all yours for the asking, and the sooner you ask, the easier your life will become. Eventually, you will overcome all roadblocks. Life is meant to be easy and effortless.

Rich is a state of mind. Nothing is impossible to the Universe. Go for the biggest brass ring you can think of. Then, get enthusiastic. If you want a mansion, write down a mansion complete with butler, gardener and cook. If you want a yacht, get the biggest and prettiest one you can imagine. This is your life. Get excited – the possibilities are limited only by your desire. At this writing Queen Elizabeth's yacht, the Britannia, is for sale. I don't think it comes with British sailors, but I am sure God can find an excellent crew. Stretch your mind. Unbridle your imagination. Reach for stars. It is this striving for your greatest possible good that allows you to grow. In fact, unless you reach beyond your current material situation you will not grow to meet your spiritual destiny. And it is, after all, your spiritual growth that allows you to become Rich Beyond Your Wildest Dreams.

CHAPTER 10

Top Secret

Congratulations! You have taken a huge first step. You have written down a number of things you want to have in your life. As you think of other things you want to have, write them down anytime. You really only need to write something down once. The Universe keeps great records. You will, however, think of more details as time goes on. Moreover, it is essential that you continue to detail your life's desires if you want your prosperity to grow. You must continually create a bigger and better success story. Every new success is simply the foundation for a greater one. You are an unlimited creative being. Why stop with a car, a house or a mate?

Reach for your notebook and write on a regular basis. Your 79-cent notebook is your blueprint for success. Use it often. I keep my current one open on my desk at work. Simply glancing at the pages of my desires helps stimulate their creation. You do not even have to read them, although you can. I just turn the pages and my subconscious goes to work. No one, however, comes snooping around in my office. If you do not enjoy that kind of privacy, keep your 79-cent notebook where no one will see it but you. The things you have written down are for your eyes only. And for good reason.

People who do not understand this system of working are often skeptical, even cynical. Their conscious and even unconscious feelings can generate negative reactions toward your success. Remember we are all connected subconsciously. If someone were to read your book they might feel jealous or angry that you have the courage to ask for the kinds of things they themselves long for. If they do not understand, they may feel obligated to straighten you out. Show you the awful truth, reality, as they see it. This is exactly the wrong kind of energy to have surrounding your blueprint for success.

Even people who do understand this system of gaining wealth – and there are many more of those folks every day – even these enlightened souls, have no business knowing your thoughts and plans. Their subconscious thoughts can affect you without their knowledge.

Yes, our subconscious connects us to the Creative Power of the Universe. It also connects us to every other human being on the planet. See the diagram below. What this means is that someone who knows your plans can merely think subconsciously and it affects you. Imagine that you and your wife plan a trip to Hong Kong and you tell two good friends. Outwardly they both praise and support you. Unfortunately, their subconscious may work against you. One friend may have been in Southeast Asia under less than friendly circumstances and subconsciously he thinks your plan is dangerous. Your subconscious receives the message – *Do not go to Hong Kong; it is dangerous.* The other friend may want to take a vacation herself, but not to Hong Kong. She wants to go to Egypt and see the Pyramids. Your subconscious receives the message – *Do not go to Hong Kong; it is the wrong place to go.* Before you know it you and your wife start feeling uneasy about your trip. "Maybe," you say, "it is not a good time to get away." And you cancel your trip to Hong Kong because your subconscious received messages from your friends' subconscious feelings. This is your life. Treat it with loving kindness and divine protection. Keep the things you want top secret.

Marilyn's *Subconscious Communication* Diagram

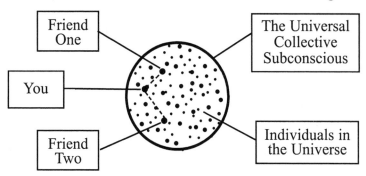

One of the best reasons, however, to keep your preferences a secret is that you actually speed up their realization. You guarantee that you get what you want faster with a higher degree of accuracy. Imagine that your desire, your creation, is a giant balloon filled with helium (spiritual energy). Once full, this balloon will carry you safely and quickly to the reality you desire. If it is a car you want, you will get it sooner. If it is a loving, harmonious relationship, you will have it now rather than later. Your act of writing down your desires has created this balloon. It has some helium in it, but not enough to get you where you want to be. Creation fills the balloon with more helium every day until it is large enough to carry you to your goal. Now, when you talk about your desires, when you share your intimate life design with anyone else, guess what happens? You let a little gas out of the balloon. Every time you say,

"I am getting a new car," more helium escapes into the cosmos. Every time you say, "I am getting married very soon," pssst – more of that precious lift is gone. Write, keep quiet and reap the rewards.

As a rule I have no idea what my wife, Diane, has written down, unless it involves me. She has no idea what I have written down, unless it involves her. If we want something we will use in common, like a new house, a vacation or our relationship, then we must cooperate and communicate or we might end up in different houses and on separate vacations.

Use your common sense. Keep in mind that this information is top secret. For your eyes only. You only need to write things down once, then glance at your list occasionally. The idea is not to ignore your desires once written, but to detach from them. You create what you want to have on paper, then you let the Universe manifest it. You still want what you want, so it does not hurt to look. Just do not dwell on how or when you will get what you want to have. Remember, God provides by means over which we have no control. Define the parameters of your desire and let the Forces of Creation do the work. This is the essence of success. This is the door to getting Rich Beyond Your Wildest Dreams.

CHAPTER 11

Detachment

Once you have written down what you want, you have a new challenge – it is called detachment. We touched on this previously. Detachment is the process of giving up what you want to the Universe. You decide what you want. You write it down, you visualize, you get excited, then you detach. You stop caring about getting what you have asked for. That does not mean that you no longer want what you asked for. You still want it. But in your heart you must not care if you get it or not. If it comes, it comes. If not, be happy with what you do have. Always be happy with your current situation.

Unless you detach yourself from the things you ask for, you will not get them. I know it sounds strange. It is one of the most difficult concepts to explain, let alone do. Yet detachment is the door through which you get everything you ever wanted.

Once you have had any experience with a two-year-old, you know exactly what detachment means. Take a two-year-old to any store and let her walk next to you. What happens? I guarantee you, sooner or later she will take off running the other way. At first, you take up the chase. You are going to catch that child and grab her hand. But guess what? Two-year-olds are fast and quick. Even if you do catch her, your success is only temporary. That ball of energy will scream and kick until you let go so she can run away again. Your little prize is playing "chase me." This is not a game adults can win. At some point, hopefully, you learn detachment. When the child runs one way, you go the other and never look back. Bingo! Your two-year-old will quickly stop running away from you. In short order she will come running back to find you. This is exactly what you must do once you have written down what you want. Turn away and the things you ask for will come running to find you.

God is the source of all your good. He is also the ultimate decision maker. If He decides you aren't ready for something yet, you won't get it. If He decides you need to wait for a few months or years, you wait. You can work your rear end off for quite a while and not get the thing you are asking for. Then when you least expect it, wham! It is yours. Why? Because you finally detached. You stopped feeling responsible for acquiring it. You stopped looking for it. You stopped worrying about it. You stopped trying to secure it by your own ability. You stopped playing chase me. You, ultimately, stopped caring about having it.

God said, "Ask and ye shall receive." He did not say, "Ask and then go get it yourself." To receive means it is coming to you. You do not have to go catch it. Delivery is included at no additional cost to you. The Universe has a distribution system that is amazing. I know this must sound strange, but it is absolutely the truth. We all grew up hearing that the early bird gets the worm. The truth is, all birds get worms. The Universe has an abundance of worms. You do not have to make any special effort to receive what you want. Ask and you will receive. It is as simple as that.

List + Visualize + Enthusiasm = Getting what you want

When you do not detach, you are telling God that you can do it by yourself. He then waits for you to do it yourself. At the very least, this puts you in the position of cleaning your house before the cleaning lady comes. Or cutting the grass just before the lawn guy gets there. Why take on all this extra work when God has agreed to do it for you? "Ask and ye shall receive."

By relying on your own efforts, you will not attain anything close to what you asked for. The difficulties you must overcome when relying on your own abilities and resources are immense. Imagine yourself trying to empty the ocean one cup at a time during a rainstorm. Individual accomplishment is an overrated value. In truth, we do not earn, achieve, accomplish, or attain anything except by the Grace of the Universe. Why fight this battle? Because your mother or your father told you to put your nose to the grindstone? Work hard and make a good life for yourself? OK, work hard, put your nose to the grindstone. I am going to Disneyland.

Write down what you want to have. Think it through. It is work creating a life. Get pictures of the things you want. Visualize your car, house, vacation. Get excited. Feel like it is already yours. Get enthusiastic about enjoying whatever it is you have asked for. Then....then do the smart thing. Detach yourself. Turn your back and let the Universe take over. Want what you asked for, but stop caring if you ever get it. This is an effortless process.

The first time I used this system it worked for me. I received in one weekend a new house exactly as I ordered it, the movers to move us there, a new car, and a new refrigerator. I had forgotten completely that I had written these specific things down only six weeks earlier. A week after we moved in it dawned on me that I had received exactly what I had ask for. I showed my wife for the first time what I had written. We looked at each other with one of those "you don't think this really works, do you?" kind of looks. See, it does not matter if you have absolute faith in this system or not. The system flat works. Fortunately for me, after I wrote down what I wanted, I gave it up to God. These were things I wanted. I never stopped wanting them. We were looking at houses when we found ours. I just wasn't expecting it. In fact, we found our house quite by accident.

Let things come to you. Look, but do not think you are going to conquer it by yourself. My daughter looked for an apartment for two months. Diane and I were constantly encouraging her to look. "Have you looked today? Maybe you should try over there. There still is a little daylight left." We were anxious for her to have her own space. She finally found her apartment coming back from the mall where she went to forget about looking for an apartment. Traffic was bad so she turned down a street she never traveled and there before her young eyes was her new home. She stopped right then and talked to the manager and within two days she had agreed to a lease.

In nature the Universal Intelligence allows birds to thrive, grass to grow and fish to flourish all without any special effort. The earth itself spins and circles the sun with no help from humankind. Nature prospers easily and effortlessly. Humans are part of that ecosystem. We, too, are destined to prosper easily and effortlessly.

Write it down, visualize, feel enthusiastic, then detach. Before you know it, many good things will be coming your way. These are the keys to that powerful Force that gives you what you want in life, making you Rich Beyond Your Wildest Dreams

I'm Rich Beyond My Wildest Dreams

CHAPTER 12

Focus on Abundance

Everyone knows that the journey of a thousand miles begins with a single step. Well, you have taken that first step and your journey has begun. This is not a quick fix or instant karma. You will learn and grow significantly if you are to acquire the state of wealth you desire. Here are a few guideposts you will need on your journey.

Live for today. Forget all the nonsense you have learned in however many years you have lived on this planet. Forget it. Many of the things you are about to learn will contradict your old-school thinking. Heck, the very idea that you can get rich without any special effort is a huge contradiction of old-school thinking. Living a successful life by this system requires a new mind set.

Focus on abundance. Think positively. Speak positively. Write positively. Believe in your success and success will follow. Remember everything is Cause and Effect.

You have a powerful new life ahead of you. You cannot afford the luxury of the dark side of life. Negative thinking, resentment, revenge, anger, fear, hatred, envy, distrust and antagonism lead to disaster. You are what you project. By allowing negative thoughts a place in your life, you set up barriers to your own good. You deny yourself the wonderful rewards that come with success and prosperity.

George Lucas is a powerful example of someone who relies on his positive force to create wealth. Hollywood is famous for gobbling up young filmmakers and spitting them out in pieces. Yet George became incredibly successful. His *Star Wars* trilogy ranks as not only one of the most successful movie projects of all time, but as one of the most successful business projects ever.

His work is totally positive. Good defeats evil in a world of amazing possibility. And although he leads us through a war of galactic proportions, there is no blood, no gore and no shocking close-ups of horrific carnage. In an industry prone to dark thinking Lucas has created action and adventure bathed in a PG rating. Men, women and children of all ages have enjoyed the *Star Wars* movies and in the process made George Lucas one of the richest men on this planet. So rich, in fact, he financed his fourth Star Wars movie himself. Giving him complete control to do anything he wants.

You, too, can do anything you want. You can have anything you want. You can be that person you always wanted to be. Simply focus on abundance and do the work described here. It is all up to you.

Close the door on your past. There is a new window open to your future. You opened this window when you took the time to write down what you want to have. Go back now and make sure you have written down everything you want. Be specific. Be thorough. Be clear and concise. Include the little things as well as the big things. Visualize having what you have written. And get enthusiastic about your success. After you have done all this, close your 79-cent notebook and detach yourself. Trust in the Force of Creation.

Let the Universe do its thing. For now you have

done all you can do. Go about your life. Then, after a while, take out your notebook and glance again at everything you have written down. Check off or draw a line through anything that you have now received.

This could be a small thing like a baseball cap or making a new friend. Whatever it is mark it off when you receive it. Then close the book. You will know when to open it again.

Stay positive. Love everyone and remember that what you project is what you receive. In fact, everything comes back multiplied. Positive always wins.

After a period of time take note of how many things on your list came to you. This is not an accident. Nor is it a coincidence. These things come to you because you ask for them. How long does it take? However long it needs to take.

At the end of this chapter close this book and put it aside until you taste those red ripe strawberries, the fruits of your labors. Then and only then will you be ready to read the next section of this book. I am serious about this. You must wait until the time is right to read further. Let me tell you why.

When I was seventeen I decided that I wanted to drive a truck in the summer. I wanted to drive an 18-wheeler. It was all I could think about. I didn't even consider the jobs that my friends took that summer. One sacked groceries. Another spent the summer nailing asbestos shingles to the roofs of houses. Another sold ice cream cones. But not me. I wanted to drive a truck.

I didn't care that the law required you to be 18 to drive a tractor-trailer rig. I was determined. I went to every trucking company in Lincoln, Nebraska, looking for a job. Most sent me packing immediately. This was a union town with plenty of healthy family men down at the union hall waiting for work. My chances were slim to none, but I kept asking. Finally, a small, independent, non-union, cartage carrier hired me to load and unload trailers.

It was hard work. I weighed about 127 pounds soaking wet and I had to move oil drums weighing over 500 pounds with only a hand truck. I went home the first day so tired I fell asleep before dinner and slept straight through until morning. I stayed with it. I was determined to drive a big truck and I was willing to do anything that brought me closer to my goal. Every morning before I punched in I would ask my boss if he had a truck for me today. He would always smile and say, "Not today, Tom. I think we need you here on the dock."

I did that everyday for five weeks. Then one afternoon my boss called me to the dispatch station. He handed me a set of keys and told me to go hook up the flatbed trailer and put it into slot 7. What a piece of cake. Slots 6 and 8 were empty. This had to be the easiest backing job a truck driver could do.

I was on fire. I was about to drive my first semi. I had finally, after five long weeks, taken the first step toward achieving my heart's desire. I was on the road to becoming a professional truck driver at the age of 17. I was ready to drive. Or so I thought.

Now, if I had been paying attention, I would have noticed the crowd gathering in the yard. Drivers, dock workers, mechanics, even several of the office crew were out to watch me back a flatbed up to the dock. Some brought their lunch. Had I noticed, I might have asked myself what could possibly be so interesting about watching me back in a flatbed. I mean, I had watched the other drivers do it. There was nothing to it.

In retrospect, I have to tell you that what was to follow was one of the most painful experiences of my life to that point. But at the time, I was so excited my feet barely touched the ground. I was "the man." The truck-drivin' man.

Well, over the next forty-five minutes I managed to destroy the bottom lights on the trailers in slots 5 and 9. I spun the steering wheel one way then the other. I drove forward. I backed up. I popped the clutch time and time again. I killed the engine. I started over. I tried again and again. The sweat poured off my body as the gathered crowd roared with laughter. I was the best joke of the year. The kid who would drive a truck was failing miserably. In the end all I wanted to do was get out of that rig and go find some corner and die.

I finally got the flatbed near the dock. It was at nearly a forty-five degree angle. But that was as close as I had been all afternoon. I set the brakes and stumbled from the cab. My truck drivin' days were over. History. Yesterday's news. Those characters in the yard would have to find other entertainment. I was quitting. What the heck. I was only 17. Obviously, I had bitten off more than I could chew. I could ignore the cat calls from the crowd. I would simply walk up to Stan and quit. They needed another sacking clerk at Safeway anyway. Truck driving apparently was not my destiny.

That's when Bob, six-foot, seven-inch, two hundred and sixty pound Bob, an over-the-road driver, grabbed me by the back of my neck. I tried to tell him he had the wrong guy. That I wasn't a truck driver after all. That I was off to easier pastures, but he wouldn't listen. He practically threw me into the cab of that International Harvester. He closed the door and stood on the running board, looked me in the eyes and said, "Now, I'll show you how to do it. You wouldn't have paid any attention before. My guess is you have probably used up most of your ideas by now and you'll listen." With Bob's help I had that flatbed squarely in Slot 7 before the crowd could dry their laughing eyes.

It is hard to digest everything at once. Learning takes time and you just started a brand new system for acquiring wealth. Give it a chance to work for you. Relax and let your body digest these new concepts while the Universe goes to work. It is always a good idea to taste the fruit before you make a pie. This is exactly the way Marilyn taught me. She wouldn't tell me everything the first time either. Consider waiting as your first exercise in detachment. Seriously, put this book down and wait until the time is right before proceeding. You have plenty of time. You'll know when. There's no rush. You have already stepped out the window and you are well on your way to getting Rich Beyond Your Wildest Dreams.

Keeping Your Prosperity Alive and Well.

It's time to let the Universe work for you. Time to open up and let your good come to you. Time to receive the things you've asked for.

Please wait a period of time before proceeding.

I'm Rich Beyond My Wildest Dreams

CHAPTER 13

Divine Timing

By now, hopefully, you have already received some of the things you asked for in your 79-cent notebook. For some people these things come quickly, for others it takes a little longer. The reason is Divine Timing.

I know a woman who was in her late thirties, never married and really had very little experience with men. She wanted a new car, a loving intimate relationship and a new job. One week after our first meeting she had precisely the car she described, with the exact terms she requested. Three days after receiving the car, she met the man she eventually married eight months later. Oh, she also quit her job and moved to the East Coast with her husband where she found a better paying job she absolutely loves. I was particularly amazed at the speed with which she got every-thing she asked for.

Everything that we ask for comes in God's time, not ours. The Universe responds at the correct time for all con-cerned. If the Creative Forces decide you are not ready for the things you are asking for, then you could have a bit of a wait. I always include many little things that I want, but which never seem to get high on the priority list, like a wax job for my car, an oil change and a steak dinner. Little things can come quickly and often provide excellent encouragement, helping to generate the big things.

Big or little does not matter to God. The little things keep your enthusiasm high, but the big things do come. Sometimes they come miraculously. Miracles are, after all, normal and commonplace. When I began writing this book I started to have back pains. My office chair was actually an old style manager's chair. It looked good and was plenty comfortable when I leaned back, but leaning forward to write for long periods caused my back to hurt. I needed a chair, but I did not feel good about spending reserve money on a new, good-quality task chair at that time.

This went on for a few weeks until I realized that I had not asked for a new chair. I had not written the chair down on my list. Writing down what you want must be done continuously. If you stop asking for new things, you stop receiving new things. It is not necessary that you write down the same things over and over again. Once is enough. As you grow, however, you need to write down the new things that you want. I included a new chair that day on my list.

After writing down my new chair, Diane and I went to lunch. On the way we drove by an office furniture store and stopped just to see what they had. I found a chair that gave me such relief, I did not know how I could go back to my office without it. The chair was nearly $600. More than I could spend. Then, as my wife and I were trying to figure out how to make the money work, the saleswoman said, "Why don't you take that chair to your office and try it for a week or so? If you like it, you can pay for it then."

I ended up trying several chairs, one after the other, until I found the right one. The miracle is, I had a comfortable chair two months before I had to pay for it. Plenty of time for God to give me the money. The Universe knew I wanted a chair and provided it for me immediately. It was easily paid for and it was the correct chair for me. I considered this a big request at the time and thought it might take a while before I received my request. God saw things differently. Not only did He provide me with the chair immediately, He provided me with the chair through a means over which I had no control. I would have never believed that a furniture store in Southern California would give me a chair to use free for two months without even taking my credit card imprint. But they did. Why? Because God is in charge, not us.

Everything we ask for comes in God's time, not ours. Do not be discouraged if some of the things you ask for take a little longer. Then again, things you do not expect arrive sooner than you could ever have believed possible.

The bottom line here is you are really not in charge. You must give up all control if these success secrets are to work for you. And if that isn't startling enough, wait till you hear the secret that guarantees your success, the number one key to becoming Rich Beyond Your Wildest Dreams.

I'm Rich Beyond My Wildest Dreams

CHAPTER 14

Guarantee Your Success

Until now, everything we have talked about centered on what you want to have. But as you probably already figured out, life is not as one-sided as saying, "I want. I want. I want." You cannot go to the grocery store and get a week's groceries simply by telling the clerk you want these things. You do not build a long-term loving relationship by focusing exclusively on yourself. Life is a two-way street and there is a cost to everything. We pay for our groceries with cash, check or credit card. We pay for our relationships by giving of ourselves. We also pay for everything we receive from the Universe. One way or another we always pay.

Paying the Universe is not a new concept. A few thousand years ago people made sacrifices of lambs and cattle, giving God His portion of their wealth. Abraham, in fact, was willing to give his only son as a sacrifice. Today, we are not called upon to make quite the same sacrifices. Today, we are called upon to give money to the Good Spiritual work of the Universe.

Over the centuries, many divine teachers have come to the various peoples of the world. Abraham, Krishna, Zoroaster, Buddha, Moses, Christ, Muhammad, the Bab and Baha'u'llah have each and every one said the same thing. Give back to God a portion of what you receive. We call this tithing.

Before you pay any bills, before you put money in savings or pay taxes, you owe the Universe. Since all our good comes from God in the first place, it makes sense that we owe Him for what He has given us. You pay the grocery store for the food you take home. You pay the hairstylist who gives you a new look. You pay the real estate agent who sells your house. God is the source of all your good. The Guiding Force of Creation has given you everything. It has given you the food you eat, the house you live in, the livelihood that sustains your life. You owe everything you have to God. Giving back a portion of what you receive is more than good manners, it's a Universal Law. You owe the Universe 10%.

You can have anything you want in this life and all that is expected of you is that you give back a relatively small percentage.

Tithing is the single most important thing you can do to guarantee your success.

Tithing means giving 10% of your gross income back to God. Before anyone else is paid, you owe the Universe 10%. This is not a bill. This is not something you can negotiate or postpone. Ten percent of your income does not belong to you. It is given to you in trust and you get to decide WHERE it goes. But you do not get to decide IF it goes. The tithe is God's money.

One story demonstrating why we give 10% goes like this. The one (1) represents male energy and the zero (0) represents female energy or the field of infinite possibilities. Since life in this world is dependent upon both male and female energy, we are employing the basic elements of Creation by using the number 10 as our tithe. Ten is the exact representation of creation numerically. You can think of it as the male (1) impregnating the female (0), so the Universe can give birth to those things you wrote down, your desires. Marilyn calls this cosmic fertilization. By paying your 10% tithe you are guaranteeing delivery of what you want. See the diagram below.

Marilyn's *Cosmic Fertilization* Diagram

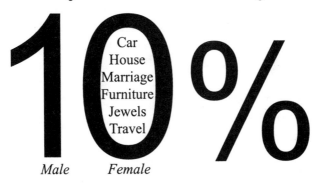

As with all things in this life, you do have a choice. You can choose not to pay God His portion. There are, however, consequences for this action. God will take His portion anyway. Remember the money is not yours to keep. You may get fewer bargains when shopping. You may have to pay full price for everything. You may experience loss in one form or another. You may be the one pulled over for a ticket even though everyone on the road is speeding. You may have your house broken into and robbed. You or your life partner may get sick on vacation. A misunderstanding may strain your love relationship. Your tire could blow out at 60 mph. It could cost you a chrome wheel, a fender, a headlight or even prevent you from reaching the meeting where you were going to make a big commission or meet the man of your dreams. The problem with not paying the Universe is that the Universe takes Its portion anyway. Often you end up paying more. And you are supporting the dark side of life. What was P.T. Barnum's favorite line? "You pays your money and you takes your choice."

By tithing to the Good Spiritual Work of Creation you are guaranteeing that you will succeed. First, your 90% goes farther. You find bargains. You pay less for the things you do buy. The thief who was casing your house is frightened away. A tow-truck pulls in front of you, slowing you down and foiling the radar cop you never saw. You and your partner are so healthy you get a reduced rating on your insurance premium. A potential problem in your love relationship disappears because you remember to bring flowers. You may do your checkbook at the end of the month and find an extra two or three hundred dollars. It sounds impossible, but this has happened to us. We subtracted properly, the bank said no mistake was made and we had more money. There is so much money in the world, it has to go somewhere. When you tithe, your money goes farther and success seeks you out. That new job, that business opportunity or that new friend you want to meet suddenly shows up in your life. Good things happen to those who tithe.

Tithing also protects you financially, emotionally, spiritually, and physically. The "slings and arrows of outrageous fortune" seem to bounce off before they get to you. You are surrounded by the protecting white light of God. You meet people who help you unravel difficulties and resolve your afflictions. You become stronger, dependent only upon God. Your life is enriched in every aspect. God takes care of His best customers.

Look at the YOU PAY ANYWAY diagram below. Above all things is the one and only Power of the Universe.

This power can be either Plus(+) or Minus (-), Positive or Negative, like two poles on a battery. In our diagram, the left side represents the Positive. The right side represents the Negative. Positive qualities of this world are listed on the left while negative qualities are listed on the right. At the bottom of this diagram is 10% of your income. When you tithe, your money supports the positive qualities on the left. When you do not tithe, the Power of the Universe takes the money from you to support the negative qualities on the right. YOU PAY ANYWAY. Fail to tithe and you invite loss, pain, failure, and heartache into your life. Pay God His 10% and you open the door to profit, happiness, health, joy, success and love. By tithing you are allowing yourself to receive the benefit of all the good the Universe has for you.

Marilyn's *You Pay Anyway* Diagram

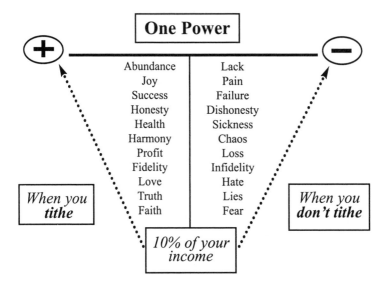

Caution! Where you tithe can be as important as tithing itself.

Send your tithe where you feel you receive spiritual guidance and the effectiveness of your tithe increases. If you do not feel a spiritual connection where you tithe, you are not receiving all the good you are due. Tithing is for your benefit. And let there be no mistake, tithing works. As long as your intent is to pay God that which is rightfully His then your tithing is acceptable. You are fulfilling your obligation. But if you are not at the same time supporting the source of your own spiritual growth, you may not be getting the greatest personal benefit.

You came into this world to grow closer to God. To gain the qualities and attributes that allow you to make spiritual progress. You are here to learn and grow. You are not here to make spiritual progress for others. They must do that for themselves. Create in yourself a pure heart and you will help humankind in the process.

You do not need to belong to a church, a synagogue, a mosque or any organized religion to tithe. In fact, the idea is to support the Good Spiritual Work of the Universe. So, contrary to what anyone else may say, you do not need to send your tithe to an institution of any kind. It may not be tax-deductible, but that's not the point. It's not your money in the first place. Your tithe is God's money. Send God's money where you feel it will promote the Good Spiritual Work of the Universe. In addition, if your tithe supports the source of your own spiritual growth, enlightenment, inspiration and help, so much the better. The important thing to remember is you can send your tithe to anyone. This can be an individual. It can be an organization. It can be a group of individuals or an institution. It can be any-where you feel your tithe both promotes the Good Spiritual Work of the Universe and helps with your own spiritual progress. Certainly you may tithe to a religious organiza-tion; I just want to make it clear this is not your only option. In fact, if you send your tithe to a religious organization from which you no longer receive spiritual inspiration or support, you are not supporting your current spiritual growth. It would be like paying money to one grocery store, but taking your groceries from the store across the street. Where you tithe is your responsibility. God wants you to decide who you feel is doing the Good Spiritual Work of the Universe and support them. If you are not sure where to send your tithe, ask God to make it crystal clear to you. You will receive direction.

You get to decide what you eat for dinner. You get to decide who your friends are. You absolutely get to decide for yourself where you send your tithe. Send it where you feel it should go. Not where you think, but where you feel it should go. Follow your feelings. The Universe directs you through your heart. Open your heart to God and you will know where to send your tithe.

Your tithe must, however, go to a spiritual source. Sending your money to the local zoo, for example, is not really supporting God's work. Unless, of course, you believe that the zoo promotes the Good Spiritual Work of the Universe. Tithing is all about your spiritual growth. Giving to good causes is an excellent thing to do, but it is not tithing. It's charity. Tithing is giving back the 10th por-tion of everything the Universe gives you. God makes it very clear to you through your feelings where He wants His money to go.

Tithing is fun. Since the amount (10%) is predetermined, it is never a question of how much you send, but only where you send it. My wife and I look forward to writing these checks more than any of the checks we write. We thank God and bless the recipient of every tithing check we write. For us, this in itself is an uplifting and inspirational experience.

OK, I hear some of you saying, "How can I give ten percent of my money back to God when I don't have any now? That's why I bought this book." This is exactly the reaction my wife and I had when Marilyn told us we had to tithe if we wanted to stay successful and keep getting the things we asked for.

I grew up in a Lutheran Church and I remember all the rich people who would talk about tithing at the annual meeting on the church budget. I guess I figured you had to be rich to tithe. My parents gave money every Sunday, but they never tithed. They thought they were doing all they could do. They never did grow rich.

Like most people I had it backwards. You don't tithe after you get rich. The secret is that you tithe and then you get rich.

Give to God out of love. He has loved you enough to give you everything you have. Give back to Him in the same spirit. The Universe wants you to be rich, so you should expect to receive what you ask for. Keep in mind your list is a list of preferences and the Universe has the final decision. God acts as your agent. He gets you work, cars, relationships, and you pay Him 10%. You are not investing to make money, you are paying back money that never belonged to you to begin with. Ten percent of everything you receive belongs to the Good Force of Creation. Write those checks first and enjoy the experience. Tithing, as with all Universal Laws, is for your benefit. Open your heart and let the good come in.

Oh, another thing, be careful of automatic withdrawal. The idea of tithing is that you are making the decision to give. It is usually better to write the check yourself every month. You are doing this out of love. Stay actively and personally involved with your tithing.

How then do you start tithing when you aren't making it now? In the beginning both my wife and I were uncomfortable with giving 10% of our earnings away before we paid bills. Frankly, we weren't sure it would work. If we gave away the 10% we already had allocated to other needs, we would be going in the hole. We'd been struggling for many years. We didn't have decent furniture, or pots and pans, dishes or even a good bed. These things had all worn out. We needed dental work and our kids were now in college and they needed help. We needed every penny of our income and then some. Give 10% away? How?

What is important is your intent. God knows your situation better than you do. Start by giving what you can. At first, we tithed less than 10% of our income. Gradually over the months we raised this amount until it reached 10% of our gross income. God allowed us to grow financially in those months and we continued to raise the percentage. Again the important thing is your intent. If you intend to give 10% and you work toward that end, God will reward you. If however, you start by giving less, but never get up to the 10%, then your good will suffer.

Tithing is the single most important thing you can do to guarantee your success. YOU PAY ANYWAY. Give 10% of everything you receive back to God and you will prosper. It's a Universal Law. Tithe where you receive spiritual growth and your success is guaranteed. Do this one thing and you will assuredly grow Rich Beyond Your Wildest Dreams.

CHAPTER 15

Your Success Covenant

Open your 79-cent notebook to the blank page you left at the very front. We are going to write your Success Covenant. Turn to the page directly across from the inside cover where you wrote "All this by Divine Right, Divine Inspiration, Divine Intervention, Divine Timing and with Good for all concerned." The Success Covenant begins your list of preferences. Normally, you write your Success Covenant and then write your list. We did it in reverse order for learning purposes. Purchase several 79-cent notebooks after you have learned this system. This notebook is for practice. I have a notebook exclusively for my Success Covenant and master list. I detail the things I want in another notebook.

The Success Covenant is perhaps the most important entry in your book. You are making a contract with your boss, your agent, your manager, your client – the source of all your good. You are going to agree on the terms of your success. This statement is derived in part from the *Holy Bible,* Genesis 28:22.

On this page write the following words, exactly, unless you want to change God to read Great Spirit, Universe, Force, Creation, etc.

Success Covenant

Dear God (Universe, Creative Force),
Thou art my master planner and partner. Of all that
Thou shalt give me I shall surely give the 10th unto
Thee. God (The Universe, Creative Force) is my
agent, my employer, my manager, my client, my boss
and the source of all my supply.

Sign your name and date the agreement.

It is important to start a new notebook after you have learned the system. Write everything in order. First, write your protection disclaimer. Secondly, write the Success Covenant. Thirdly, write your master list of preferences or requests. Fourthly, in another notebook, write the details of what you want.

Here is the reason you write a list of the things you want immediately following your Success Covenant. You are making a contract. You are telling the Universe that you will give back 10% of everything you receive. In return you want the things on your list. Cause and Effect. You pay and you receive. It is that simple.

This whole process of tithing and receiving is, once again, very much like a trip to the grocery store. You make out a list of the groceries you want and you send someone, your agent, to the store in your place. Naturally, you give that person money to buy the things on your list. The grocery store is not about to let anyone have the groceries until they are paid for. You do not get something for nothing in this world. By the same token you do not expect your agent to hand the clerk money and leave without your groceries. You pay money and you get what you want. Tithing is the same way. God is your agent and you agree to pay him a set percentage of your income. In return, He gives you the things you want. Yes, you have to pay 10%. But you can ask for absolutely anything.

Your Success Covenant is your contract with the Creator. It makes clear exactly what you owe and it spells out exactly what you want to make you Rich Beyond Your Wildest Dreams.

I'm Rich Beyond My Wildest Dreams

CHAPTER 16

Thank You. Thank You. Thank You.

Giving is the key to receiving. If there is only one thing you get from this book, let it be this. Let me repeat that for you. Giving is the key to receiving. This is so very important. I cannot overstate this golden bit of wisdom. If you do not write anything else down, if you think all the rest is hogwash, if you think you'd rather put your nose to the grindstone than follow the suggestions in this book, fine. Just do yourself one favor: Give. Follow this one piece of advice from this day forward and success will come to you in abundance.

Creating a cash flow is nothing more than increasing the income you receive on a regular basis. With this system of gaining wealth that is very easy to do. Simply give more and you will receive more.

Certainly, tithing is giving. It is your gift of thanks to God. Tithing, however, is more like a commission you owe regardless of whatever else you do. Tithing gets you into the school of success. Giving freely to others, on the other hand, sets you at the head of the class.

Giving money and resources away out of love and kindness is a very powerful thing. It is, precisely how the Universe functions. God gives you everything. He gives out love and kindness. How could He not reward your doing the same thing? When you give freely to others you activate the Law of Tenfold Return. It is like seed corn. You plant one kernel back in the ground and get a manifold increase. This Law is set down in every major religion in the history of mankind. It means that when you give one dollar freely to someone else the Universe rewards you by returning to you at least ten dollars. You give one, you get back ten. You give five, you get back fifty. You give one hundred, you get back one thousand. Give a million, get ten million. There's no limit, because you cannot out-give the Universe. What happens is that your giving creates a vacuum which the Universe must fill. Isn't that one of the things you learn in high school physics? "Nature hates a vacuum." Your giving creates a hole that must be filled. This is not some form of idealism, this is a Law of the Universe. You give money, you get money back, multiplied ten times. Period. It always works. Drop a pencil and it falls to the ground because of the Law of Gravity. Give money away and you get money back because of the Law of Tenfold Return. Naturally, the time and method for returning this tenfold payment is up to the Forces of Creation. You will, however, usually see a rather quick turn around. Which makes this a fantastic way of generating income. All you have to do to get it is to claim it. Give freely and claim your reward.

Marilyn told me a story about giving in Las Vegas. She used to host bus tours for seniors going from Orange County to the action and excitement of Las Vegas. On one such trip Marilyn overheard a woman say that she wished she had some more money to play, so Marilyn gave the woman ten dollars. The woman was one of the folks on the bus tour and didn't want to take the money. Marilyn told her she could not refuse her gift. That, of course, would hurt Marilyn as well. The woman did take the money.

Marilyn turned around and put a quarter in a slot machine. She won $100. A tenfold return, exactly. Then, she scooped the quarters up and took them home in her purse because she didn't know the casino would cash them in for dollars, but that's another story. The point is that by giving the ten dollars away she created a vacuum which the Universe immediately filled with a tenfold return.

You are undoubtedly giving already. Every time you eat in a restaurant and leave a tip for the server you are giving. The standard tip is somewhere between 15% and 20%. My guess is that you are not claiming this gift. I wasn't. Didn't even think about it. I considered the tip part of the cost of having dinner. It is not. You are giving. If you pay $30 for dinner and you leave a $5 tip, claim it. Pay the bill, walk outside so no one thinks you have lost your marbles and say out loud, "Thank You. Thank You. Thank You, for the fifty dollar tenfold return."

It is not just a good idea, it is the law. The Law of Tenfold Return. For every good that we give, we receive a minimum tenfold return. For every hour of comfort and love we extend to a friend, we get ten hours of love in return. Maybe not from that same person. Maybe we get our ten hours from someone else. All our good comes from God, remember. He determines when, where and how we receive. The only thing that matters is that we give so that we can receive.

The next time you find yourself low on funds, give something away. Give money to a homeless person. Give money to a friend for no reason. Tell them you want to increase your cash flow. Give money to a school activity. Pay your gardener more than you owe. Tell him thanks. Leave a few dollars in the tip jar the next time you get a bagel or coffee. The money will pour in. You have created a vacuum which the Universe must fill. Clean out your closet and give the clothes you do not wear to a charity or someone who can use them. Before you know it that void in your closet will be filled with brand new clothes. I gave away an old computer to a friend and within a few weeks I had more than enough cash to buy a bigger faster one. Giving generates income.

Sometimes the value you receive in return is beyond dollars and cents. I never will forget one Christmas I spent in a hotel in Phoenix, Arizona. Our family and Diane's sister's family were attending a conference as an excuse to meet half way and enjoy the holidays.

I was always missing the lectures, usually for a very good reason, like watching the Lakers play the Phoenix Suns. Well, after the game I left my room and headed across the street to another hotel where most of the formal meetings were held. It was cold. The wind was blowing and I saw two men, both haggard and dirty, walking towards me. They walked past several people from the conference, but those folks were in a hurry to get inside where it was warm and they paid no attention to these two needy men.

Soon we were face to face. They were gaunt and their faces were marked with deep lines. They had very little hope in their eyes. It was obvious to me their lives were much harder than my own. They asked if I could spare a few cents. I was there on borrowed money myself. My life was less than prosperous and I had long ago resolved not to give money to the homeless. Heck, they would probably just buy alcohol anyway. So I had my head down and I, too, was ignoring these two men. Then, I do not really know why, maybe I figured a bottle of cheap wine would be better than nothing on a night like this, maybe love for the human family grabbed me, I do not know why, but I stopped, turned around and called to the men who I had already passed. I gave them a couple of dollars, not much.

It was the light in their eyes that I remember. They had hope. They smiled great toothless smiles and thanked me, profusely, for my gift. They said that my gift gave them just enough for a room for the night with a bowl of soup. They were serious. They blessed me and wished me a Merry Christmas as they hurried off. I stood there with tears in my eyes, thanking God that their plight was not mine and that for the first time in years I had done the right thing.

Those other folks who had ignored these men missed out on quite a reward. Oh, by the way, someone bought our dinner that night. Something I hadn't counted on. It kept me from running out of money on that trip.

Marilyn has a great rule of thumb for giving to the needy. "You never know," she says, "that one of the poor and hopeless people you run into aren't angels sent to test you."

I like to think that the poor in our midst are our trust from God. This, too, is supported by holy writings, but there is one rule of thumb we can all follow:

When in doubt, give. It only makes you richer.

A few months ago my oldest daughter, Penelope, went to the post office to mail a few letters. There is a dirty and tattered man who usually sits by the front door. He never asks for money and most people never even see him. He's part of the landscaping, I guess, like a broken bird bath. As everyone else had, she walked past this man on her way in. Suddenly, she realized that he wasn't asking for money. Why was he there every day? Certainly there were more exciting or more comfortable places to sit.

On her way out she stopped and looked at the man and said, "God bless you, man." As he looked at her through his sad, painful eyes, a smile of relief came to his face. "Thank you," he said. "You'll never know how much that means." We have not seen that man at the post office since.

Give and you will be Rich Beyond Your Wildest Dreams. Give and you will receive at least a tenfold return. Sometimes the return is priceless.

My wife has given $35 every year to a Shakespeare festival in LA, even when we didn't really have it, because she wanted to. The production raises food for the homeless and gives "at risk" kids in gang areas a chance to see the beauty and the mastery of a professional Shakespearean production.

Now, I think we give $100, but the point is we have received inestimable returns on that gift. Every year we celebrate our wedding anniversary with front row seats for a superior Shakespearean production. We usually take ten or fifteen friends, eat a picnic and enjoy a great evening under the stars. How do you value that return? In LA that kind of seating could easily cost $200 each. Our guests and we are treated like royalty. We help the homeless by bringing canned food and give thousands a chance to watch a play written nearly four hundred years ago by one of the greatest masters of all time. They watch for free. We get to be royalty. What a deal.

Remember to give, then claim your return. Leave a $5 tip and say, "Thank You. Thank You. Thank You, for the $50 tenfold return." Give a friend who's having trouble $20 and say, "Thank You. Thank You. Thank You, for the $200 tenfold return." Drop a couple of quarters in one of the charity boxes in the grocery store and say, "Thank You. Thank You. Thank You, for the $5 tenfold return." Always say "Thank You" three times, there's power in it.

Once you start giving and claiming your reward, the money will begin to come to you. Tithe on that money and more money will come. Give away more money and even more money will come to you.

If you go to lunch with someone, buy their lunch. Then claim your tenfold return. If their lunch costs $10 and you leave a $3 tip, say, "Thank you, thank you, thank you for the $130 tenfold return." Next week your friend may buy your lunch. If he offers, accept. Tell him to claim the reward. Giving becomes addicting. You'll feel great about the act of giving and you'll see more money coming to you.

Oh, one more thing. Money coming to you can also mean not spending as much. Once you start tithing and giving freely, you'll see a wonderful result. You'll find things do not cost as much for you. The things you want may be on sale. Or someone gives you exactly what you need, before you even know you need it. Marilyn gave me a copy machine. I didn't need one at the time, but I am not about to refuse a gift. That stops your good from coming. Later I needed a copy machine. I had it for free. Marilyn got a $10,000 tenfold return for giving me the copier. This is a good deal.

Giving is a win/win scenario. The giver wins a tenfold reward. And the recipient wins a gift. The more we give, the more we receive. So, give freely and claim (out loud) your tenfold return. You will, absolutely, grow Rich Beyond Your Wildest Dreams.

CHAPTER 17

Having Fun

You have written down what you want to have. You have tithed on your income. And you give freely to your fellow humans. Now what? What is next? What else do you do to insure the acquisition of all you have asked for? The answer is perhaps shocking – have fun.

Part of this system is to enjoy what you do have. Worrying only produces negative results. Whatever you worry about, you create. Not a good direction to go. The opposite of worry and concern is a carefree confidence in success. Believe in your own success. Have fun. Enjoy yourself. God has given us a world of fun things like the beach, Disneyland, movies, skiing, cruises, fishing, hiking, camping, baseball games, football games, ping pong, croquet, plays, concerts, card games, computer games and, of course, my personal favorite, basketball – everything that is fun for fun's sake. Get out and do things. All work and no play makes you dull and boring.

This concept carries over to your work. Find the things in your work that give you pleasure. Most people are attracted to a particular kind of work because they enjoy a certain part of it. Then the politics of the workplace take over and, zap, you end up doing things you hate. This is not beneficial to your success. Sure you may have to continue to do things that are not exactly what you want to do, but you probably can focus on the things you want to do. If not, if everything about your work is distasteful, maybe you had better take out your 79-cent wide-ruled, spiral notebook and ask for a new job. The Universe will grant your request.

Write down the circumstances surrounding the situation you want to have. If you want to be an artist, write down the things you have in your job: flexibility, security, time off, fun people, creativity. Write down that you use your artistic abilities, that these abilities are appreciated, that your work is fulfilling, that you have a large, steady, dependable income. Your new job will find you or the old job will improve.

We work better and we are more productive when we are happy and having fun. Maybe you need to take some time off and go have fun. We do. Every once in awhile we will close the office and take the whole staff to a special outing. The first time we did this we all went to Disneyland. It was a great success. It gave us a chance to detach ourselves from the work in the office. We stopped thinking about all the problems we needed to handle, all the reports that needed writing and all the calls that needed to be returned. We had fun and let the Universe do its work without our interference. We turned our back on the business, so the business could come to us.

Have fun, it pays.

A few years ago I met a man in Las Cruces, New Mexico, who said something about enjoying your work which touched my heart. When I met this man he was 74 years old, wealthy and still actively selling very expensive fire alarms through dinner parties. He would go to a town and get someone to invite all his friends to a steak dinner at the local steak house. He bought you a steak dinner and all you had to do was watch a 20-minute presentation on fire alarms. Which, of course, scared the dickens out of everyone. Then he made an appointment to come to your house where he sold you $2,000 worth of fire alarms.

I do not personally like this kind of selling. It is definitely not for me. Sure, people probably need the product. Maybe he even saved more than a few lives through his efforts. But he was rich beyond my dreams and for the life of me I could not figure out why he continued to do this work – work I would personally find unrewarding. His answer surprised me.

He said, "I do it because I enjoy it. A man is a fool to do anything other than what he enjoys. Work is where we spend most of our time. If you do not enjoy what you do, you better find something you do enjoy quick. Life is too short."

I left New Mexico within three months and quit the life insurance business altogether. I went to California to write screenplays. I wrote three and sold one which was not produced. I struggled financially. Still, that was the best move I ever made. That move led me to where I am today. I didn't stay with screenwriting, but that doesn't matter. I took action. I did something that I wanted to do. Like Robert Frost said, "I took the road less traveled by, and that has made all the difference."

Had I not come to California in search of a dream, I might not have written the screenplays that prepared me to write this book. I might not have met Marilyn. I might not have worked though the pain of my emotional and spiritual lessons. I choose to live authentically. Oh, if I could give you this feeling I have right now, you too would choose to live authentically. There is no substitute for finding your success, the road to your destiny. We all have one. It's just a matter of finding it.

The road to your success begins with a simple self-directive – have fun. Enjoy your work. Enjoy your play. Play often. Most of us grew up with the concept that we must work hard to succeed. And while it does take effort to live your life, it is just as easy to have fun as not. Take time off in the middle of the day. Go to a movie or watch a baseball game. Focus on the things in your work that give you pleasure. Open your heart to the fun all around you.

Enjoy yourself. Life is too short. What did Christ say? "This life passeth quicker than the twinkling of an eye." Nobody ever expected you to live this life in pain and misery. Certainly not God. He wants you to be happy. "Thy kingdom come,... on Earth as it is in heaven." Certainly, heaven is full of joy and happiness. The happier you are the more prosperous you will be. Wealth will seek you out. Success will call your name. Next to tithing, having fun is the single most important thing you can to do to insure your prosperity.

Of course, that does not mean you will have one day of ease followed by another day of ease. You will invariably go through many tests and difficulties in your life. The trick is to know in your heart that whatever happens you are safe and protected. That the Creator of the Universe did not create you to be a slave. That you are to fulfill a greater purpose. The trick is, regardless of your situation, have some fun.

At the very least you can go for a walk, or read a book, or talk to a friend, or paint, or throw a party. You can grab a hunk of cheese and a little bread and go have a picnic. Meet a friend and go window shopping, or play golf, or bridge, or write your own book. There is something you want to do. Something you think of as fun that you are not doing now. Do it and watch the value of your estate rise.

If tithing is the heart of success, then having fun is the breath that brings your success to life. Have fun in work. Have fun in play. Have fun and become Rich Beyond Your Wildest Dreams.

I'm Rich Beyond My Wildest Dreams

CHAPTER 18

Faking It

Who are you? Are you a winner? Are you a loser? After reading this far in the book do you know who you are? Are you a strong, powerful, positive-thinking, motivated, self-starter? Or are you an average person who wants to improve your life? Are you the person you think you are? Are you the person everybody else thinks you are? Are you the person you always dreamed you could be? Or are you really faking it?

There is a common virus persistent in our human family. It is the virus of doubt. It whispers in your ear, suggesting you are not as successful or as powerful or as loving as you want to be. Or that you are lying to yourself and to others about who you really are. At times we all feel like we're only pretending. That we are not really the person we want to be. That we are letting ourselves or somebody else down. That we are not living up to our image or potential. And I am here to tell you that these things are simply not possible.

You are who you are. You are a valued member of the human family. You are one of the nearly six billion men and women on this planet. You were put here for a reason and the rest of us need you. Even if some of us forget sometimes, we still need you. We need you as much as your heart needs your lungs, or as your electrons need

113

your protons. You are part of the single universal soul of this planet and we need you. God loves you. And if you simply ask, the Great Spirit will send all the help you need at any time and under any circumstances.

Not believing in yourself is a form of fear. And fear must go so that your good can flourish.

Think about the times you felt pressured or upset while you were working. How many of these instances relate to your fears? Are you afraid you will displease someone? Are you afraid that you will not measure up to the job? Are you afraid you will get criticized, yelled at, or fired? Are you afraid you will let your team down? Cost the company or yourself money? Or perhaps show everyone you are not the person they think you are? Are you afraid you are not the person you think you are?

This is absolutely not possible!

You are a unique and select individual. You are a specific combination of molecules, electrons, protons and energy which is not duplicated anywhere on the face of this earth or any other planet in the cosmos. You are unique. There is nobody like you. The Law of Probability determines your singularity. It is not even remotely possible for you to have a duplicate. Identical twins are not truly identical. And even if some mad scientist should some day find a way to clone you, you and your clone would, from the instant of his or her creation, be different. You would have different perspectives, different experiences and different desires dictated by the fact that you each have separate and distinct lives. You are like no one else. You can only be you.

The thoughts and desires you have belong to you. If you think you can heal people, you can. If you think you can win the lotto, you can. If you think you can meet and marry the person of your dreams, you can. If you think you can grow Rich Beyond Your Wildest Dreams, you can. You can do it, because you possess the thought. This is a very important concept. Remember it. The thought of a unique individual by definition is unique to that individual. And the potency of that thought is inherent in having the thought.

More simply, whatever you think – you can. In fact, you would not have the thought if you did not have the capacity to achieve it.

If you can think it, you can have it.

You are designed by nature to be self-fulfilling. Every aspect of your creation is propelling you toward achieving the very thoughts you often think are beyond your grasp. You are designed to fulfill a purpose and your mind knows it. Trust yourself. Believe in yourself. Do the best you can. Ignore those who would make you doubt yourself. Bless them for they are filled with negativity and cannot follow you. They question your ability because they are not sure of their own.

Cause and Effect – everything you put out comes back multiplied.

Sure, you may have to learn a lot to get where you are going, but you are destined to get there, which means you are entirely capable of learning the lessons. You may fail to achieve ends that were not for you to achieve, but those very failures propel you toward your true self.

Can you guide a large rock stuck in the mud? No. Imagine that same large rock rolling down a hill. Now can you guide it? You can push it one way or the other. You can decide right or left while gravity does the rest. This is one of the secrets to your success.

Can the forces of the Universe guide you if you are standing still or stuck in the mud of fear and indecision? No way. You must be moving before the Universe can guide and direct you toward your desired end. Remember:

Nature guides a rolling stone.

Imagine that the person with whom you are the closest is hurt and needs your help. This person is trapped in an abandoned mine several miles from the road, across a desert canyon filled with rattlesnakes, scorpions, cactus and all manner of deadly peril. It is 130 degrees outside and you must leave now to save your friend before he or she dies from loss of blood. You have no choice. You must go.

Imagine also, that since it is your destiny to save your friend, the Universe will guide you through this valley. Even though you are careful, how do you know where the sleeping rattlesnakes lie? You don't. But the Universe does. Perhaps you scratch your leg on a cactus and as a reaction you move more to the left and there you see a wider path which you follow. By doing this, the Universe has steered you away from a rattlesnake, a danger far greater than the cactus. You can be guided once you begin your journey. This is the way of the world. We take action, the Universe guides us.

"Do something even if it's wrong," a friend from Texas used to say. By the time he was thirty he had over a million dollars in the bank and was married to one of sweetest ladies I had ever met. He started with nothing except desire. He was determined to be rich and he followed the Universal Laws.

He sold real estate as an agent until he decided that

he could make more money buying and selling houses. At that point he returned his real estate agent's license to the state. He felt it was morally wrong for him to negotiate to buy houses from people without declaring his license. So, he chose to go through a period of time without a cash flow, without monthly income. It was hard, but he made it. And he tithed on the money he made. From then on he was the Teflon investor. No matter what trouble beset those around him, he came out of it clean as a whistle and richer than ever. He knew that he was destined to be wealthy because he believed God had created him with that potential. He followed the Universal Laws and he trusted in his own feelings. The deals came to him. He was prosperous. He was happy. He was simply himself.

Forget the garbage you have learned your whole life. Forget that you are supposed to struggle and work at a job you do not love. Or that you must work like a slave. Forget that you have to prove yourself or live up to other people's expectations. Trust in the Universe to guide you. Know that you are the one and only you. Know that you are who you think you are and you can do whatever you think you can do. Know that your thoughts are not only important to you. They are important to the rest of us. Write them down and make it so. We need you to be Rich Beyond Your Wildest Dreams.

I'm Rich Beyond My Wildest Dreams

CHAPTER 19

When the Rain Sets In

Picture yourself in a verdant garden. Everywhere you look there are beautiful and exotic flowers. Lucious fruit of every variety hanging ripe on the trees; scores of vegetables, plump, juicy and delicious, all within arms reach. Picture yourself in a garden filled with everything you ever desired. Blue sky up above and birds chirping in the warm sun. This is heaven on earth. And you can have it for the asking. Whatever you want you can have. Just remember one thing-this is still the planet earth and sooner or later the rain sets in. The skies will darken as clouds cover the sun. Lightening and thunder will quiet the birds and for a while it may seem as though the sky is falling. It may seem as though all your rich dreams are about to come crashing down around you. You may even feel like you are making a huge mistake, that everything you've learned here is wrong and leading you down the path of destruction. The truth, however, is something else entirely. The truth is you're in for nothing more than a little wet weather.

Imagine that you have written down everything you want. You have visualized yourself enjoying these things. You have gotten enthusiastic about actually having these things in your life. You have detached yourself from caring about ever having them. You tithe on a regular basis. You give freely of yourself to others. You have freed your mind of negative thinking. Love is your favorite color. And now despite all this, just when everything looked so promising, all the trouble you could possibly imagine comes knocking on your door. Why?

We live in a world governed by natural laws. The foremost of which is cause and effect. For every action there is an equal and opposite reaction. Growth is organic. Growth requires change. If you ask to grow big and strong, don't be surprised when the rain sets in.

The process of change that must first occur before you can have the prosperity you desire is called Chemicalization. It is the stirring of the pot that makes the soup. It is an actual chemical change. Chemical change is necessary for creation. Water, for example, is a combination of hydrogen and oxygen. Separately, they are two gasses; together they make a liquid. All of creation, including you and me, is made of chemicals. If you are not rich now and you want to be rich, then you must undergo a chemical change. By definition you want to be different than you are now. The things around you must also undergo a chemical change. This is as basic as life itself. We call this process Chemicalization.

Sometimes this means that the situation you are in will change dramatically. Your business will take a sudden, unexpected drop. Old friends will leave and relocate somewhere else. The one you thought would be your partner for life falls in love with a fishing boat and sails into the sunset. Things change. It is, after all, the only constant in this life. Whether you know it or not, your written list of preferences is an order for change. An order that has a potency as absolute as any seed planted in the ground. But before your order can grow tall and strong it needs rain and fertilizer. That means you may get wet and you may even step in something nasty.

Chemicalization is merely a restructuring of your situation. It does not mean the other shoe has fallen and that you are bound to fail. It does not mean that you are being punished for your sins. Or that any number of negative thoughts have any validity whatsoever. This is nonsense. It is always darkest before the dawn. Chemicalization simply means your plans are working. That your gold is being washed from the dirt. That your crops are growing and the harvest is assured.

Remember, all of your good comes from God. He will never throw you to the wolves. He is rearranging your life to make room for the things you have requested. There must be a winter before there can be a spring. You have redefined yourself. You have spun a cocoon by asking to be rich and now you are changing into someone you always knew you could be. You should expect a hard rain now and then. It is all part of the process of cause and effect that underlies all life on this planet.

Not long after I started using this system I learned about Chemicalization, up close and personal. I was selling advertising for a technical web site. Sales were booming. Every month I sold more ads for more money than ever before. My relationship with the client got better and better. I was the fair-haired hero. I could do no wrong.

I decided to put this system of creating wealth to work in a big way. I wrote down the parameters of a huge successful business. I spent my savings on new equipment and I added the monthly expense of a new salesman. My ship was coming in and I wanted to be prepared. My expenses grew to an all-time high, yet I figured I would probably retire within a year. The Web site owner started talking about going public. I was in high cotton when the rain set in.

121

One night in June the server crashed and we lost all our data. The backup failed and we could not restore a thing. A Web site is nothing but 0's and 1's. It is digital information stored electronically. It had taken our programmers and developers a year and a half to create this modern day marvel and in a couple of nanoseconds the whole thing was a memory. It was less than a puff of smoke.

Well, it does not take a genius to know you cannot sell much advertising on a non-existent Web site. I worked harder than I had ever worked in my life just to stay alive. My survival and the very survival of the Web site was dependent upon keeping the sponsors paying. This was not easy. Every day I came to work and faced a growing discontent among those who had paid for advertising that they were not getting. This lasted for nearly two months. At that time I could not have told you one good thing that was happening to me.

Marilyn told me it was Chemicalization. She told me not to worry. She said I should write down more things I wanted to have. Give me a break! The water was up to my neck. What I needed was a big boat. Maybe an Arc like Noah had. What I failed to realize at the time was that my 79-cent spiral notebook was my big boat.

Because of the Chemicalization on our Web site, we rebuilt bigger and stronger than ever. We threw out old technology and rebuilt with new innovative techniques. Since we were not burdened by some of the old cumbersome methods, we created a whole new site which was faster and more effective than ever. In fact, because of the Chemicalization we were forced to create a Web site that was actually capable of meeting my aggressive new goals for growth. The old site would never have allowed us to grow as fast or as big. Our sales skyrocketed and by the end of the year we had surpassed my own projections. All this because the rain set in.

Change, however, comes from two sources. In addition to Chemicalization, we must also deal with Mr. Negative. Mr. Negative is fear. Our own fear that we are not who we believe we are. That we do not deserve the Good we have asked for. Mr. Negative wants us to fail. He wants us to quit. He wants us back in leg irons, enslaved by the tedium of yesterday's reality. He wants us to work long hard hours, to scrimp and save and struggle to pay our bills. He wants us to lose track of the prize we have set for ourselves. To stop planning for success and accept defeat.

Fortunately, Mr. Negative is weak. He works hard, very hard, but he is not nearly as strong as your Positive side. He can get you to make mistakes. He can make you question your own Good. He can sometimes convince you that everything you believe is a lie. He is full of logic and reason, hate and anger, jealousy and rage. He is everything negative and desperate, but he is weak. If you bring a lamp into a dark room, you get light. If you bring a bucket of darkness into a lighted room you still have light. Mr. Negative is doomed to lose. He will lose, because you have an invincible protector waiting to carry you safely through any attack. You have an impregnable stronghold waiting to insure your victory. You have the force. You have the unlimited power of the Universe at your fingertips.

The secret to dealing with Chemicalization or Mr. Negative is to keep your cool. Take a deep breath and say out loud, "This too shall pass." Relax and trust that the Universe has your best interest at heart. No matter how bad it gets or how much it hurts or how dark things look, you must trust in your own inevitable success. A success guaranteed by the Prime Mover Himself. These hiccups are merely the ups and downs of life's cycle. Whatever you do, do not quit. Do not give up on yourself or on this system of wealth and happiness. Do not give in to the dark side. Mr. Negative only goes to work because you are ready for a big increase. He is afraid you are going to leave him behind. He is fighting for his existence. And there is an easy way to let him slip into the void where he belongs.

When the going gets tough, ask for more stuff.

Grab your 79-cent notebook and write down more things you would like to have. Marilyn is right. Asking for more good will remind you that you live in a diamond mine – not a mere hole in the ground. Focus on the Good you have. Focus on the Good you want to have. Stormy weather is merely a confirmation that you are set to grow even richer. Picture having everything you have asked for. Imagine the fun of driving your new car, living in your new house, cooking dinner with your new mate. Get excited about having the things you have asked for. The Universe wants you to succeed. In fact, your success is already fixed like one of the stars in the night sky. Even when you cannot see it, you know it is there.

If the rain sets in and you need to talk to someone, talk to us. From time to time everybody needs help. Send us an email. The email address is in the front of the book. Email only, please. It is so much easier for us to respond to an email. We will respond to you. In fact, we would like to get to know you. You are one of those lucky people who are Rich Beyond Their Wildest Dreams.

CHAPTER 20

The Help Button

We live in a computer age. Every day we become more and more dependent upon computers. Personally, we write letters on the computer, then send them via email over the Internet. We can read our morning news online. We can buy flowers, order books and invest in stocks with the click of a mouse. All this, however, is possible because of one feature in all computer programs. This one feature allows us to learn how to use our computers without doing any serious physical damage when the frustration builds. When you do not know what to do, you can always click the Help Button.

Using this system for getting rich, you undoubtedly will find times when you simply do not know what to do. You may feel overwhelmed, frustrated, beaten, discouraged, angry, picked-on, deserted, envious, depressed, despondent, attacked…. You may lose your perspective. You may start listening to Mr. Negative, who can be a very persuasive little stinker. You may find yourself in the middle of a period of Chemicalization and just plain lose it. When this happens, when you feel like you need help – use the Help Button.

Write a letter to God. This is your ever-present Help Button. It is guaranteed to work 100% of the time.

When things are not going well, when you have no

idea how to solve a problem, when your boss or your mate becomes irrational, when you are buried under a mountain of bills – write a letter to God, the Power of Creation, the Good Force of the Universe. This is your greatest Friend. This is your Sustainer. This is the One who gives you everything. Who wants you to succeed. Of course this Universal Omnipotent Force will help you. Keep your letter simple and to the point. Explain the situation as you see it and ask for HELP. Then thank your Benefactor in advance for taking care of your problem. Here is a sample letter if you need one. I always write to God. You could as easily write Dear Universe.

> *Dear God,*
>
> *I need your help. I feel pressured by my boss to work longer hours without extra pay. I don't think that's right. I have a family and he doesn't. I want to go to soccer games with the kids and have an occasional date with my wife, but I have bills to pay. I can't afford to lose my job. What am I supposed to do? Please make it very clear to me beyond a shadow of a doubt what I am to do. Thank You in advance for your help.*
>
> *John*

Remember to sign the letter and then put it in a safe place. Or tear it up and throw it away. This is between you and the Power of Creation. No one else need be involved.

Keep in mind that you are writing this letter to your best and dearest friend. Pour your heart out. Say anything and everything that comes to your mind. When I first started doing this I was very frustrated and angry about a particular situation. So I blamed the Universe. I wrote that I felt that He really let me down. I asked Him to tell me what I was supposed to do. I detailed the problems I was having and signed off. Well, I felt better right away. Immediately, I felt relieved of my burden. I had expressed my true and honest feelings and my Best Friend had listened and helped. I don't recommend you make a habit of blaming your tests and difficulties on God. These are your tests. I'm only pointing out the power and the freedom you have when asking for His Help. The Universe knows your situation better than you do. He made you rich and He will come to your aid when you ask. The point is you can be yourself. Be honest. Express your feelings. God can take it.

Now, some people like to destroy their letters to God after they write them. I do not. But then I still have papers I wrote in the late 60's in a box somewhere. You can tear up the letter. You can burn it. You can wad it into a little ball and shoot baskets with it. It does not matter. The Universe got the message. Help is on the way.

Oh, it goes without saying that once you write your letter, you must detach yourself. If you ask for help, you have given up control. Sure you want the problem solved, but if the solution does not fit your preset notion of how things should go, so be it. The Creative Forces of the Universe managed to work out gravity, sunlight, oxygen, all those things that keep us alive. They can handle your problems. Write and detach.

One couple I know live on the east coast in a rented house. They have a fledging chocolate business in their home. Great chocolate. Well, she called me one Saturday morning to say that her landlord had just given them notice to move. They wanted the house back. She was torn apart because she had planned to stay in this house and eventually buy it. Besides they had moved so many times, they were tired of it. She wanted to know what she could say to God to get this all straightened out so she could stay there. Well, I suggested she write a letter to God and give Him the problem. In the end they found a new house which is bigger, and has everything they need for their chocolate business. Remodeling the old house would have cost them $25,000 out of their own pocket. In the new house it was already done. The Universe knew their situation better than they did.

Recently, Marilyn's landlords decided to get serious about selling the house she had lived in for years. Actually, Marilyn and the couple that owned the house were good friends, so Marilyn agreed to stay while the house was shown. She liked the house and didn't really want to move. In fact, the house had been for sale for several years with no takers. So Marilyn figured that the Universe would make it crystal clear when it was time for her to move. The landlords made sure the real estate agency who listed the house knew Marilyn was a friend. The agency promised Marilyn they would call ahead 24 hours. They also promised to follow Marilyn's one request that everyone remove their shoes at the front door. Well, it didn't work out quite that way.

The listing agent would show up without calling. Actually he was doing what real estate people do. He was selling the house and he had to show it when the opportunity arose. Of course, these people paraded through the house without taking off their shoes, constantly interrupting Marilyn's work. The intrusion became overwhelming. Marilyn felt like maybe it was time for her to go, so she went into her bedroom and wrote a letter to God.

Dear God,

I can't do my work with this house thing going on.
If I'm supposed to move, please take care of it.
Fix it. And I want white carpet in the new house.

Thanks,

Marilyn

About ten minutes after writing the letter, one of Marilyn's clients called to thank her for the help Marilyn had given her. That client was also a real estate broker. Marilyn told her about the difficulty she was having and the broker said, "You know I just took a listing on a rental this morning. It has a fantastic view of the ocean, but it does have one drawback. White carpet."

Within twenty-four hours Marilyn had seen and signed a lease on that very property. Naturally, the old landlords were a bit shocked by the swiftness of her move. Marilyn was out within two weeks. She has a newer house with an incredible view of the Pacific Ocean all because she gave her problem to God. Oh, the old house sold to that last prospect and the new owner was thrilled to take possession immediately. Things resolved with good for all concerned.

No matter how difficult things are. No matter how overwhelming the situation may seem. You always have a place to turn. Use the Help Button and write a letter to God. It's fast. It's free. It's one of the many gifts the Universe has given us to insure that you can grow Rich Beyond Your Wildest Dreams.

I'm Rich Beyond My Wildest Dreams

CHAPTER 21

http://www.richdreams.com

What you are learning here is powerful information. This is the same information Moses, Christ, Baha'u'llah – all the Divine Messengers and potent philosophers of history have set down for our growth and understanding. These are the practical applications of the Universal Laws of this world. They are at times a mystery, an apparent contradiction of all that we have learned from our parents and teachers, a paradox of this reality. Now, I am not here to prove these laws nor to even recite them all; that you can do when you write your book. What I am here to do is to explain how you can use them to get Rich Beyond Your Wildest Dreams. Follow this path and you will open the door to your own prosperity. You will swim in a sea of wealth and happiness. Trouble will no longer harass you. Living your life will become a joy you never dreamed possible.

How many times have you been told that nothing really changes in this life? That might makes right? That power is as power does? That the rich get richer and the poor get poorer? That bankers rule the world? That what's good for big business is good for you? That it takes money to make money? Oh, and of course the golden rule of the business world – gold rules? Well, forget it. Throw away your old concepts of wealth because we are entering the Age of Aquarius. This is the beginning of a new world order. A world order in which "the first shall be last and the last shall be first."

The age of competition is over. Look around – it is dying everywhere. And in its place you will see the beginning of the age of cooperation. Perhaps the place to look first is the great equalizer, the common people's window to the world. That amazing storehouse of information and opportunity which is even now eclipsing television as the dominant medium of the twenty-first century.

Welcome to the World Wide Web.

It took radio 33 years before it had 50,000,000 listeners. It took television 13 years to raise 50,000,000 viewers. The Internet already has 50,000,000 people online less than five years from the beginning of commercialization.

In the fall of 1997 there were 27 million computers connected to the Web. By March of 1998 there were over 50 million computers logging on, surfing, downloading, researching, investigating, buying, selling, chatting, sharing, communicating openly and freely without prejudice for reasons of gender, race, nationality, sexuality, religion or ethnic background.

This is the beginning of a revolution that will help bring peace and prosperity to the world community. For the first time in our history, the people of the world are connected to one another. Free to share information and friendship across continents, across oceans, across party lines, across borders, across misinformation and diplomatic maneuvering.

What did W.C. Fields say? "You can't con an honest man." Well, the Internet has just given us the opportunity to all become honest men and women. We can know through our own eyes and not through the eyes of others. We can find and know the truth for ourselves.

If you have not yet experienced the Internet, do what millions of people everyday are doing – shut off the TV and log on. Find out for yourself what everyone is talking about. See why nearly every TV commercial has a Web address listed. When I was living in Houston many years ago there was a rather arrogant local TV commercial by an oil service company. It ended with the tag, "If you don't have an oil well, get one." Then, it was arrogant because the average person watching that commercial was locked out. Not everyone could get an oil well. It can easily cost over a million dollars a day to drill for oil – that's after you own a lease and have the necessary government permission. Today, you can have the equivalent of an oil well for the price of a home computer. Any average person can get on the net and do amazing things.

I have for years relied on a particular man to clean our carpets. He is a good worker and does a great job. I trust him and wanted to help him get more business. So the last time he did our carpets, I asked if he needed a list of my friends to prospect. He declined, said he was cutting back on the carpet cleaning business. He said he was spending more time buying and selling currency on the Internet. What!? Yes, my carpet cleaner guy has a program that helps him make extra money buying and selling foreign currency on the Internet. He said he is really conservative and only makes about $300 a day working an hour or two in the mornings. That's more than $70,000 a year. A lot more than he makes cleaning carpets.

Another friend of ours is an attractive woman in her early forties and the mother of four. She recently divorced her husband of twenty-fours years. They parted as friends and she's lately been searching for a new love relationship. This lady "chats" with men from around the world. They discuss all the things people discuss when getting to know each other. She has had dates with men from Louisiana, Denmark and Australia. She really hit it off with the Australian guy. He came to California to visit her and she's gone to visit him. Wedding bells? Who knows? Romance and the Internet are the key words here.

Success stories and the Internet are now nearly synonymous. If you are not online, you are missing the time of your life. You can visit the Louve in Paris, watch the Pandas playing in the San Diego Zoo or get the latest pictures from the Hubble telescope. You can see the price the dealer pays for your new car before you negotiate. Heck, you can get a couple of price quotes on exactly the car you want without even leaving the house. You can buy a good book or book a good trip. You can buy stocks or stock up on free video games. You can talk to someone when you are lonely. Or you can use your alone time to explore a whole new world.

Get online. If you don't have a fast enough computer, buy one. Write it down. "I have a new computer. It is fast enough and configured properly for using the Internet. I am online." Internet access will soon be a standard, much like the telephone.

Besides, if you want to ask me questions, you have to use my email address in the back of the book. The speed and efficiency of email makes it possible for us to respond to you. Or you can visit our Web site. The address is the title of this chapter. Hey, the Internet isn't everything, it's the only thing. Particularly, if you plan on getting Rich Beyond Your Wildest Dreams.

CHAPTER 22

Claim Your Wealth

Get excited. Get enthusiastic. Grab your car keys and put on your buying hat. It's time to get out there and claim your wealth. It's time to get the things you want now. Not tomorrow. Not next year. Not someday. NOW! It is time to find the house you want. Now. It is time to find the pearl necklace you cannot live without and make it your own. Now. Go directly to your nearest and finest shopping mall. Drive to your favorite car or boat dealer. Spend Sunday going from one open house to the next. You are going to shop your heart out. Because if you want to be rich, you have to claim what you want now. Right now. You are rich, rich, rich, rich, rich. Your benefactor owns the very planet you live on. He has all the money in the Universe. And He says you can have anything want. So, go claim it.

Claim your wealth and it will come to you.

Imagine that you are sitting with 20 other people in a circle around a table. In the middle of the table is a basket of fruit which the Universe has provided for you. Someone across from you picks up the basket and takes out a piece of fruit and hands the basket to the person next to her. As the basket goes around the table everyone takes a piece of fruit before passing the basket on. The basket finally gets to you and there is one piece of fruit left. There are still four people besides you without any fruit. What do you do? Do you (a) take the last piece of fruit and cut it into five pieces? Or do you (b) refuse the last piece and pass the basket on? Or do you (c) take the last piece of fruit and put the basket back in the center of the table for the Creative Power of the Universe to refill?

Make a choice before you read on.

The basket of fruit represents the bounty of the Universe. It is unlimited. This story helps illustrate the importance of trusting that God will provide for you. If you chose (a) cutting up the last fruit, then you are saying that the last four people should trust you to feed them, not God. If you chose (b) refusing the fruit, then you are saying that you are refusing the good the Universe has given you. If you chose (c) taking the last piece of fruit and replacing the basket, then you are on the right track. You are trusting in the providing power of the Universe.

Knowing that all your good comes from the Universe and TRUSTING that it will come are two different levels. Knowing is a conscious thought. Trusting is an emotional understanding and it is much more powerful. Claiming the things you want and then watching them be delivered strengthens your trust.

Trust that God will always refill your basket and you create a powerful and compelling enthusiasm for receiving. Combine this heartfelt confidence for receiving with a specific tangible request, your claim. Then you have magnified your ability to get what you want when you want it. Claim what you want and the Universe delivers.

Claiming specific items as your own creates an invisible bond between you and the items you have requested. Remember wealth is your birthright. The Universe has always intended for you to be rich. You were born rich. Part of your wealth is the God-given power to request. To ask that it may be given unto you. Claiming invokes this power. It establishes precisely what you are requesting without the possibility of error. You may ask for a blue sweater, but that is still a vague and ambiguous request. Yes, a blue sweater is not a green shoe, but there are millions of blue sweaters in the world. Claiming makes your request specific, exact. You are saying to the Universe that you want this blue sweater, right here. This is what I am asking for.

The power and effectiveness of claiming is absolutely amazing. Several years ago Marilyn stopped by a store on her way out of Chicago. There she saw a very large and beautiful polished rose quartz crystal. She wanted it immediately. Today, she calls it her pink rock. She felt like it was hers. But when she asked the price, it was more than she felt comfortable paying. So in her thoughts Marilyn said, "Dear God, I want that crystal. If it's mine, please let it wait for me." She headed for California without her pink rock.

Two years later Marilyn returned to Chicago. Again on her way out of town she stopped by that same store. And there in the window was her rose quartz crystal. Marilyn expressed her amazement that such a pretty pink rock would still be there. "You know shortly after you were here the last time that stone disappeared from the store," the owner said. "Apparently someone stole it. Then, earlier this month I stepped in the back for a couple of minutes and when I returned, your pink rock was lying on the counter. I guess whoever took it brought it back for you." The merchant then reduced the price, saying he probably wouldn't be able to sell it to anyone else anyway. When Marilyn claimed that pink rock she established a powerful and invisible bond with that specific rose quartz crystal. It was hers. She knew it. The store owner knew it. And obviously the Universe knew it. Claim your wealth and it will come to you.

You have asked to grow rich. That is a process. You do not just wake up one day and zap you're rich. That would be counter to the natural order of things. Your growth to riches is an organic change which occurs over a period of time. That means that you will constantly have to step up to a new level of wealth. Let us say that you are accustomed to spending $20 on a pair shoes. When you go looking for shoes you look at the $20 variety. Well, you want to get rich, right? That is what you asked for, isn't it? So, now when you go shopping, look at the $100 or $200 shoes. Upgrade yourself. It is all part of the process of accepting the level of your prosperity. Unless you set your sights on the more expensive things of this world you will forever stay where you are. Rich is as rich does.

Growing rich means constantly stepping up to a new level. It is extremely important that you claim the things that go with the level you are stepping up to. Stretch yourself. Get what you really want. Claim your wealth or you will not grow. If you stay at your current level of prosperity, if you get comfortable with what you have, you are telling the Universe that you really didn't want what you asked for. And you wasted your money on this book, not to mention all the 79-cent, wide-ruled, spiral notebooks you have purchased. Besides, stepping up to a new level creates even more enthusiasm.

Think about buying a new $200 pair of shoes and you get excited. Wow! You are wearing expensive shoes. It feels great. You stand a little taller. You walk a little sharper. You look fantastic. All of a sudden it hits you. You are getting richer. It's working. This stuff really works. Look at your feet. You're rich. You may feel so good you decide to go to a fine restaurant. Hey, you certainly have the shoes for it, right? Then when you get to the restaurant, do the little things wealth affords – valet park your car, order the filet instead of the sirloin, get a nice appetizer. This is how enthusiasm helps bring the goodies to mama and papa. Little by little, bit by bit, you grow into your wealth. First your shoes, then a fine dinner, then a new house and before you know it you are Rich Beyond Your Wildest Dreams.

You cannot save up for wealth. You grow into it. Accept the gifts God gives you. Claim your wealth. True security is much more than a savings account or an empty credit card. True security is much more than a retirement package or a portfolio of stocks and bonds. All these things can go away in the blink of an eye. Banks fail. Companies downsize. Stock markets crash. Even the monetary system itself can vanish into thin air. Nothing in this world lasts forever. "Yea, even the great globe itself shall one day vanish."

True security is trusting the Universe to provide for you. Always.

Trusting in God means not being afraid. The Universe is all-powerful. It gives you what you ask for. Fear is not allowed. Fear you may not be able to afford the things you want. Fear you may not have enough. Fear you may not be able to pay your bills. Fear your income may stop. When you fear the loss of money, you have made money your god. "Ask and ye shall receive." Ask that it is paid for easily and the money will come to you. Decide what you want and the money comes. Claim your wealth and it will come.

This is the point that you must understand. This is the difference that makes millionaires out of wage-earners. You do not save the money and buy the thing. You buy the thing and the money comes.

Claiming is cosmic buying power.

This is critical to your success. This concept is the gasoline that powers your new car. It is the fuel that heats your new mansion. You do not save money for what you want. You buy what you want and God sends the money to pay for it. You find and claim your house and the Universe gives you the money to close. You choose $200 shoes and the money will be there. I am not saying that you should write hot checks. I am not saying that you should max out your credit cards or go without food. I am saying that you must claim your wealth if you really want it.

Here's an example.

I collect rocks and crystals. (Marilyn's rose quartz story perked my interest.) I never collected anything before in my life and I absolutely love this hobby. I am constantly learning things and meeting interesting people who share my common interest. My wife and kids also enjoy rock collecting, although my wife's rocks are generally much smaller than mine and are set in some form of jewelry. Well, late one night I was reading about this rare stone and I decided I had to have one. It was a citrine formed on top of smokey quartz. Many people believe it is supposed to attract wealth and increase profits. My kind of stone. I have also wanted to improve the quality of my collection. I wanted a show piece. A mineral of exceptional quality. Of course, I wrote all these desires down in my 79-cent notebook. About two weeks later my wife insisted we go to our favorite rock shop. She had jewelry that needed repair.

Once in the store I saw a new specimen they recently acquired from a large private collection. Of course, it was a museum quality citrine on smokey quartz with a very hefty price tag. I loved the stone, but didn't have near enough money to buy it. I decided to wait and save up the money. Life, however, does not always work that way with this system.

The next day I realized that this citrine was my stone. I had asked for it. I had written it down and visualized receiving it. I was excited about owning it. And there it was, waiting for me to act. I hurried back to the rock shop.

I was there less than ten minutes when two other "big collectors" came in to buy this very piece. I told the owner I wanted the rock without discussing the price or how I would pay for it. The store owner put my name on it. Right then. Later, he gave me a price much lower than I expected to pay. And he put the rock on layaway for me with nothing down. I, literally, acquired the rock without any money at all. And the only thing I did was claim it as mine. The store owner offered the price and the terms without my asking.

I claimed what I wanted and the Universe took care of everything else. Claim your wealth and it will come. In fact your enthusiasm will soar and all the little difficulties of life will fade from the splendor of your success.

When the going gets tough, claim more stuff.

I have a friend, Dave, who regularly goes into a very expensive linen shop in Newport Beach. They have a set of sheets there which cost $900 per sheet. And which he has claimed as his. Once a week he goes in and touches those sheets. Now, since my friend does not even own a car or a bed large enough to fit these sheets, most people would think that he is either crazy or seriously over-extending himself. He, however, owns those sheets. He is claiming them now in full confidence that the money will come later. And the money always comes. A while back Dave introduced two men over coffee. One was an inventor and the other was an investor. It turns out these guys are, now, in the process of closing a multi-million dollar deal. My friend gets a huge finder's fee for that introduction. Something he never expected. Those $900 sheets are coming home to papa. Claim what you want and God sends the money.

Claim your wealth and it will come. Step up to a new level. Get enthusiastic about this new life you want to live. Start living that life now. Today. Go out and buy something you want. Claim your wealth and the Universe will take care of the details. God makes life effortless for us if we simply live it. Go shopping. Claim the things you want, now, and you will grow Rich Beyond Your Wildest Dreams.

CHAPTER 23

Foolish Spending

Beware! Beware! Beware! Dangers lurk in this ocean of wealth and abundance. Good people can lose their birthright. Honest people who otherwise would have enjoyed brilliant careers, happy families and lived in the lap of luxury instead bring themselves to a tragic end. They have everything and they lose it all. They lose what God has given them because they fail to recognize the dangers of spending money foolishly.

My friend, the General, reminds me that spending your money in one of the following three ways is guaranteed to carry you, sooner or later, to the lagoon of broken dreams, where the murky waters of foolish spending will strip you of your wealth, your health and leave you stranded in the boggy swamp of those who might have been. Whatever you do, please, avoid spending your money in the following ways:

1. Failing to Tithe – Spending His money on yourself.

Failing to tithe and then spending on yourself can be truly disastrous. You owe God 10% on every dollar you get. Period. It is His. Not yours. He does not like it when you cheat Him. He is doing all the work. You may think it is your genius or sweat that has created your wealth, but it is not. If you doubt who is doing the work, you can stop tithing for a month and watch your prosperity come to a screeching halt.

Remember tithing is not for God's benefit, it is for your benefit. God does not need your money. Tithing is for you. You tithe for your own benefit. You are paying for your spiritual growth. You are paying for the things you receive. You are keeping your ego in check and recognizing the source of everything you have. You are tithing because God is in charge and He expects you to. You tithe because you love God and it is good for you.

Where you tithe is as important as tithing itself. You send your tithe to individuals, groups and institutions that provide you with spiritual assistance. Send your money to those who help you grow and learn spiritually. This is about Cause and Effect again. You send the money to pay for your growth. You do not take groceries from one store and pay another. You pay where you get the benefit and you increase the effectiveness of your tithe.

Oh, here's another thing to remember. You do not tithe based on need. Tithing is for your benefit not for the benefit of the recipient. If you want to support homeless people, starving children or any number of excellent efforts, good for you. But that is not tithing. That is charity. Giving freely to others. If you want to support a religious organization you left several years ago because they have fallen on hard times, great. Do it. You'll get a tenfold return. Just do not count it as your tithe. Because it is not. You tithe where you get the benefit. Tithing is for you, not them.

Tithe 10% to God on every dollar you receive and you will be Rich Beyond Your Wildest Dreams. If, however, you decide to keep it and spend it upon yourself, He will do two things. One, He will stop giving you what you ask for. Two, He will take His 10% anyway. You will pay more for the things you want and need. Things will break down. Your wealth will decline. Your health will deteriorate, relationships will erode and your life will become more a bowl of pits than cherries.

A couple started using this system a few years ago and they did very well. They could not give 10% at first, so they gave what they could with the intention that they would pay more as their income grew. Well, they flourished and for a year they increased their tithing until they reached 10%. Then something happened, as it often does; this life is more of a test than a reality. Their income dropped for a period of time and their expenses had increased over time. They lived in a bigger house, they ate at nicer restaurants, they spent more on clothes, and on and on. So, they dropped down to giving 1% or 2% of their income. They continued with this level of tithing and, amazingly, their income continued to drop. Within six months they were considering bankruptcy and blamed this system. "Mumbo-jumbo" I believe was the term.

Fortunately, they asked for help, saw the problem and increased their tithing immediately. Their income rose accordingly.

The Universe will test us. God wants to make sure you will keep your word. Because once you stop tithing 10%, it is always harder to start again. Many, many people fail to receive their wealth for this very reason.

2. Playing God – Saving other people.

God allows no others before him. Spending to save other

145

people puts you between them and God. You are playing God. You become their savior. It is a seriously destructive practice. God will not allow it. He will take your money, your health and eventually your life.

Let us assume you have followed all the steps outlined in this book and you have a great income and have everything you ever dreamed of having. What do you do now? Now, you start paying your sister's bills. You know how tough it is and you have plenty, right? Why not help them out? Pay their house payment. Month in and month out you pay the bills that keep them in their house. Sure your brother-in-law hates his job and would probably do better if he went back to Texas like he is always talking about doing. But what the heck, you know better. Besides, your sister is suffering. She is forced to buy her children, your nephews, used clothes. You are dressing your kids in designer wear and hers are practically in rags, one step up from the poor people your church takes Thanksgiving dinner to. Why not buy some clothes, too? I don't mean for birthdays, or Christmas or just an occasional gift, but every month you take them out and buy clothes. Or maybe it is easier to simply pay her credit card bills. What can it hurt? We are supposed to give after all. Right? Wrong! Dead broke wrong.

There is a fine line between giving freely to others and playing God. Maybe God wants your sister and her family back in Texas. Maybe there's a car wreck waiting for them here, while Texas holds the key to their prosperity. Your money is the only thing keeping them here. Every sign in the world has told them to go, but you keep writing the checks. Or maybe your sister is supposed to get so frustrated that she gets a job that leads to a business from which they prosper. Maybe they are supposed to go into therapy and you deny them this natural evolution of their life. Or maybe the reverse occurs – because you buy them everything, he feels emasculated; they fight and eventually get divorced.

Whatever the outcome is for them, it is worse for you. You put yourself in God's shoes. You took His place. You put yourself before God. And what did Moses carve on those stone tablets? "Thou shalt have no other gods before me."

If you pay somebody else's bills, if you become the source of their good, you will lose your money, your health and then you'll die.

I know of a woman who learned this lesson the hard way. She had learned this system of achieving wealth and followed it to the letter. She tithed regularly, she gave freely of herself, she maintained a positive mental attitude and love was her favorite color. She and her husband had developed an excellent business, they were in good health and never wanted for anything. Then she started paying her two brothers' families' bills. Month in and month out she paid their rent and their utilities and even their food bill. She even gave them cash to live on.

This all came to light because her husband took ill. Slowly over the months his health deteriorated. He worked fewer hours at the business, he developed a strange unexplainable shortness of breath. His heart was OK, but he had no energy. He grew weaker every month as she paid her siblings' bills. Eventually, the business suffered. New business dried up. Old, long established accounts stopped buying. Within a year the business was on the verge of bankruptcy and he was in bed more days than not. The doctors had no explanation for his illness other than the modern day equivalent of "he needs a good leeching." The truth was he already had several leeches attached to his well-being.

Once this woman stopped paying her family's bills, both her husband's health and the health of their business improved overnight. Literally, the next day an old client decided to come back. Her husband's mysterious illness eventually vanished into thin air. Her two brothers and their wives took back control of their own lives and everyone lived happily ever after.

Sometimes your own children can cause you to fall into this trap of playing God. Once your kids are grown, they need to develop their own relationships with the Universe, directly. And you need to stay out of it. Everyone, even your own children, has the right to learn through their own actions (The Law of Cause and Effect). If you get in the way, you hurt them as well as yourself.

This can be very painful for a parent. Our friends had a twenty-four-year-old daughter living with them. She never could seem to get enough money to buy a car much less live on her own. Our friends knew this wasn't good for anyone. Their daughter was constantly fighting with the mother. These fights were small, annoying problems that served as a constant irritation to the entire house.

After consulting with Marilyn, our friends decided to charge their daughter room and board. It gave her a sense of worth she did not have before. She also got used to paying rent. On a higher scale, she was asking the Universe to provide her with rent money. By paying her parents rent, she created a category for rent which the Universe filled. Almost immediately she began making more money at work. Many of the problems at home went away. She flat made more money and had more fun. Within months this girl bought a new car, found an apartment and moved out.

Playing God is a very bad idea. It hurts everyone involved. It stagnates your spiritual growth and creates an effect which can cost you everything.

3. Hoarding – Saving for the wrong reasons.

Save for the wrong reason and the money train runs out of gas. The concept here is hoarding. Loving the money more than its source. Remember the root of all evil is love of money. God wants you to trust in Him, to love Him above all things. When you horde, you are placing your faith and trust in the money you have saved. You have put money above the Good of the Universe. You are saying that no matter what happens you will have the dollars or pesos or yen you need to handle it. Which simply is not true. You cannot possibly save more money than God can take away. You are not as powerful as the Universe. Think of the Titanic. It was designed to be unsinkable. The safest ship to ever sail the ocean blue. It was thought to be so safe that they didn't even take all the life boats on its maiden voyage. They left them back on the dock in England. It took five years for men to design and build the unsinkable Titanic and about two hours for the Forces of Creation to turn it into a rusting hulk on the ocean floor. The Universe is more powerful than anything you can devise. Hoarding means you are asking God to prove His power. Bad idea. Very bad.

This does not mean you cannot save money or invest or have retirement plans. All these things are well and good. It is the excess we are talking about. And, as usual, the most important aspect is intent. What do you intend to do with the money you are saving?

If you are hoarding money, squirreling it all away for a rainy day, watch out! The first thing that will happen is a downpour. You will get what you are preparing for. Every thought is a command. If you are saving for hard times, the subconscious produces exactly what you are most afraid will happen – hard times. Those rainy days will come and you may very well be washed out to sea.

Spend your money wisely and avoid the quicksand of spending foolishly. Tithe first with the first check you write. Do not under any circumstances play God. Save, but do not horde. Spend wisely and you most certainly will be Rich Beyond Your Wildest Dreams.

CHAPTER 24

Good Wins

By now you may be asking yourself a good question. I know I would be. The question is what about all the people who got rich by less than highly spiritual methods? All over the world there are people who use others, abuse others, dominate, lie, cheat, steal, engage in all manner of disreputable businesses and business practices and they got rich and powerful doing it. Why? Why is our system of gaining wealth valid and the opposite not valid? Why are they allowed to embrace the lower qualities of man while we are discouraged from it?

We have to think well of everyone. We bless those we would rather hate. We have to remember that everything we say or think comes back to us multiplied. Cause and Effect. If we yell at a driver for cutting us off on the freeway and make some angry disparaging remark, then we, in truth, become the recipients of that bad will – ten times stronger than we gave. Why are we held so accountable and these otherwise-oriented folks do whatever suits their fancy and they grow richer and more powerful every day?

The fact is, regardless of what we read, hear or think, we have absolutely no idea whatsoever how anyone else lives his or her life. What someone does in private can be exactly opposite of his or her public persona. We simply do not know what really happens that allows people to get rich. That is one reason why "How I Got Rich" books are so popular. Nobody knows what the other guy is doing. What you do is between you and the Universe. Some people follow the Universal Laws instinctively. It comes naturally to them like walking or eating. It feels right to them to do the same things some of us have to learn. We all come into this world with different lessons to learn. Some people know how to get rich from the start. The bottom line is you never know another person's lesson. You never know why or how someone else got rich. You would have to live in their shoes every second of every day and then you still would not know, because each of us has the privacy of an individual soul.

There is, however, another reason why this system of acquiring wealth is so important. We are about to enter a new millenium, a new age in the evolution of humankind. The times they are a changin'.

As we move closer to the turn of the twenty-first century, we watch the old world order change. Already we have seen the death of communism in the USSR. Remember the USSR? Remember the cold war and the incredible fear of nuclear holocaust? Remember the Viet Nam War and Afghanistan? Remember the local good guys defeating the big bad war machines from the super powers? Certainly you remember the crumbling of the Berlin Wall on the nightly news. Things have already changed dramatically and it is only the beginning. What is that quote from the Bible? "The first shall be last and the last shall be first."

Money has a power and those who have achieved it by other methods than those described here are numerous. But those avenues to success are closing. Even if you want to get rich by hook or by crook, your chances of success are slim to none. There is a changing of the guard. Instead of the good dying young, it is time for the good to win.

Keep in mind, also, that a law is a law. If it works for one, it works for all. The money laws work no matter what else you do. If a Mafia don tithes, and gives money away freely, then he will have a tenfold return. Now, his personal relationships may not work well for him. He surely will have to work harder to protect his own life and the lives of those close to him from the horrors he is dishing out. Yes, he'll make money. He probably will not have as much free time or nearly as much fun. Along with his ill-gotten gains, he has acquired an unhealthy debt. We are all accountable to the Universe for our actions. Cause and Effect. What goes around comes around. I do not want to wear those shoes, do you?

A word of caution! Hating the rich and powerful for not doing good is a very dangerous attitude. By damning them you dam up your own good. Those who have obtained wealth by scurrilous means are really doing the best they can. They do not know another way. This has worked for them and believe me if you had achieved wealth by other means you would not be reading this book. You are not here to judge anyone. Judging others does nothing to benefit you. The fact is, hate is hate, and what you put out, you get back. Multiplied.

Besides, is it not easier to love everyone and let God do the work? Accept it. God does the work. We may earn our living by the sweat of our brow, but the Universe gives us the opportunity. He makes it possible for us to have the work. Is it so hard then to believe that our work really is worship? That by praising God, living a good life and tithing on every dollar of income we are simply allowing the Universe to fill our cups until they run over? It is a very simple system.

The Economics of Good are powerful and sure.

As an example of success of the economics of good, I offer a controversial figure – Ross Perot. To some he is a hero, to others he is a kook. Believe what you will about the man. You can believe that he is a nut, as both the Republican and Democratic parties like to characterize him. You can believe that he is strong-willed and bull-headed. You can believe that he had ulterior motives for running for President. No matter what you believe, the fact is he started with nothing and now has several billion dollars. The fact is that he tithes on every dollar of income. The fact is that he is loyal to his people and believes in the greater humanity of man. Ross may be a nut, he may be extreme and fundamental in following the Universal Laws, but whatever else you say about him, realize how he got rich. The source of his wealth is the same as yours.

Ross has given huge amounts of money to charity. He personally financed attempts to free P.O.W's of the Viet Nam War long before our Washington politicians even admitted there were any. He organized and funded the only successful rescue of Americans from Iran during the American Embassy Hostage Crisis in the early 80's. And regardless of your political views, it was primarily his money that financed his Presidential campaigns. His political debt was nil.

You can criticize Ross till the next tax hike, but you must admit Ross Perot follows the Universal laws and now he is a billionaire. He is one of God's best customers. And God takes care of his best customers. Ross Perot is an excellent example of new age success. His wealth is derived from good.

154

Good is not popular. Mr. Negative is popular. He works hard at being popular. He wants you to believe in lack and guilt and unfair play. Because those things keep you enslaved to failure. They fill your days with drudgery instead of fun. And they keep you from claiming your birthright of wealth, happiness and good health.

This time around good wins. Believe it. Buy it. Own it. You do not under any circumstances have to hurt others to get ahead. God will give you everything you need for incredible success if you just let Him. The Universe needs your success. It needs good decisions and good actions driving the behavior of the world. One good success breeds a chain reaction of good success. The world needs more Good Guys.

I remember this film about science that was shown over and over again while I was growing up. It was shown on TV. It was shown in the classroom and it was shown in assemblies. I cannot forget it, actually. The show demonstrated very effectively how a chain reaction works.

Someone had placed about ten zillion mouse traps in a room. Each mouse trap was set with two ping pong balls (twenty zillion balls total). The narrator tells how, once started, a chain reaction grows exponentially. It gets faster and faster as each new reaction is triggered. To demonstrate, the narrator throws one ping pong ball into the mouse trap/ping pong ball reaction thing. Wow! At first, the reaction was slow, only two balls popped up from the one, then four, then eight, then sixteen, then thirty-two. Eventually all twenty zillion ping pong balls were triggered. The room was a blur with white ping pong balls.

Right now, you can be one of the first to ping the bell of outrageous success. Your success can trigger a couple more, and those a couple more and so on and so on. You might think of what you are doing as building a spiritual multi-level business. Getting rich can be a "cause." Or you can just enjoy giving and receiving good. Either way you get to live a rich, joyous and healthy life.

Relying on this method of success means you do not have to look over your shoulder every time a car backfires or go white when a highway patrolman pulls alongside your car. You do not have to drink Maalox when the IRS wants you to stop by for a visit or stare at your shoes when a street person stands next to you with a sign that reads, "Will work for food." There is no success more rewarding than one you can enjoy all the time. That is, truly, Getting Rich Beyond Your Wildest Dreams.

CHAPTER 25

The Big Game

Ever wonder about the meaning of life? Ever wonder why we are here? Why we are born? Why we sleep, eat, reproduce and die? Ever wonder what the reason is that we grace this particular planet with our presence? Well, part of the answer has been in our literature for centuries.

It is all a game. Life, death, wealth, poverty – it is all a game. A real game with your will pitted against your prejudice and your fear. You and Mr. Negative slugging it out in the age-old battle of Good over evil. He wants you to quit. He wants you to believe that truth is a lie. He wants to get into your head and destroy your hopes and your dreams. Do not let him. He is scripted to lose; you have seen or read the story many times. Good always wins. The only way to fail is to stop trying, to quit, to do what Mr. Negative wants.

When the going gets tough, let God take over. He is your guide, your protector, your agent, your employer, your client, your lover, your friend, your counsel, your everything. He is the very definition of success. Write down what you want. Visualize it. Stay detached. Get enthusiastic. At all times you must stay happy and enthusiastic. Love the life you have. Forget the small stuff. You are here on this planet to learn qualities that will lift you up and carry you forward.

It is not an accident that you want the things you want. This is all part of a greater Universal Plan. You are here to learn specific lessons. Those lessons can be represented by a certain level of material gain. As you learn these lessons you acquire the material things associated with each lesson. Material possessions are relatively unimportant in this life. You can, for example, live your whole life and never ride in a motorized vehicle. The Amish do. They ride in horse-drawn carriages. They have no electricity, no televisions, no washers and dryers, no telephones or computers, and they live very satisfying lives. We need food, water, shelter and clothing. That's it. Love helps, of course. But for all practical purposes we do not need the material things of life. Yet, even though material things do not matter, it is absolutely necessary to have the things we want. Because having those things is integral to learning our lessons.

A new car, for example, means nothing. It is ultimately a smelly, noisy, rusting hunk of metal destined for the scrap heap. It is the lesson that we learn which allows us to have the new car that is important. The new car is nothing, but having it means we have learned who we are. It is a reflection of our progress. It makes our lesson real. If you are worth a new Mercedes Benz S600, why not have one? If material things do not really matter, then it does not matter either way. You may as well have them as not.

You desire the things you want because of the lessons you must learn to get them. This is the secret to having everything. This is the essence of the power of acquiring wealth. Want it. Visualize it. Detach from it. Accept it. Open your heart and let the energy of the Universe flow through you. Become a hollow reed and feel the power of Creation flowing through you.

At the same time, you must not expect to receive what God does not want for you. You may ask for something which requires a lesson you are not yet ready for. Regardless of what the Universe sends your way, know that what you receive is exactly what you need at that point in time. Trust the Force of Eternity to promote your best interests at all times.

How often do you think back on your life and recount the hard times you went though? How often do you laugh at the victories you won against seemingly impossible odds? Every gathering of old friends or family enjoys a retelling of the tales of younger years and lessons learned. Why should today be any different? Why should your lessons today be any less arduously fought? Would the 1998 Super Bowl victory by the Denver Broncos be as sweet for John Elway if he had not lost three times before?

Ask for the things you want. Detach and give them to the Universe. Then live your life with every ounce of courage, love and enthusiasm you can muster. Enjoy this moment in time; it will come no more. Today's lesson learned becomes tomorrow's fading memory. By reading this book and following its suggestions you have discovered the Heavenly Garden of Wealth. I invite you to enter and join us, to inhale the fragrance of its beauty, to stay and tend the garden for life.

You are a fantastic creature. Part animal, yet primarily a spiritual being connected to the Universal flow of consciousness. Your job is to enjoy the thrill of victory and the lessons learned. Love every minute of your life and you are always the victor. You are forever Rich Beyond Your Wildest Dreams.

CHAPTER 26

The Invisible Path

Congratulations. You are still with us. Apparently you feel this system of success is for you. Or, at least, you are willing to give it a try.

Now, we step off into the wild blue yonder. We grab hold of that ever-present challenge to your success. We must confront the single biggest reason for not maintaining your success once you find it-your ego.

Success is a journey. Along that journey you find many new and exciting gems, treasures, storehouses of truth and wisdom. Sure, you think you are looking for diamonds, rubies and emeralds, but these are only physical manifestations of spiritual realities. Trinkets that proclaim to the world your success in overcoming seemingly insurmountable odds, to snatch victory from the jaws of defeat, to learn the lessons God has laid upon your path.

We might as well start with the number one lesson in everybody's path. Not all paths have the same lessons, but there is one we all have in common. We must each and every one learn that the All-Encompassing Power of Eternity is supreme. Not us. Though we may feel God's presence inside us, we are not God. No matter what your ego says. You are mortal and all that you have or ever will have comes from the Universe. Not from you or anything you do.

The ego comes in two separate but equal forms. The first ego form is the I ...as in I did it all. Everything I have I earned myself. I pulled myself up by the bootstraps. Nobody did this for me. I worked my fingers to the bone. I struggled. I fought the battles. I won the victories. I took the bull by the horns and made my success. I built this business with my own two hands. I found my wife and gave her everything she has. I made him what he is today. My husband was nothing before I met him. I gave you the money that allowed you to succeed. I supported you. I brought you into this world and I can take you out. Obviously these I tantrums can go on and on and on.

The second ego form is the Not I...as in I cannot do anything. I am not worthy. I am not doing everything I should do. I am not working hard enough. I am not a good father. I am not supporting my family well enough. I am such a failure. I am a poor lover, mother, sister, brother, husband, son, daughter. I never learn. I always make mistakes. I am not who I thought I was. I am letting others down. I always seem to make the wrong decisions. I am poor. I am a pitiful excuse for a human being. And on and on and on.

Yuck. I do not know which is worse. Actually, they are equally disgusting and they are exactly the same thing. They are commands. They both say, "I am more powerful than God." Both take the Universe out of the Provider role and replace it with you and your limited resources. Thinking you are greater than God is a huge mistake. The first ego says, "I can do it all," while the second is saying, "I can undo it all." I am more negative than God is positive. Wow. Think about that. Either way you are putting yourself before the All Powerful Force of the Universe. You are saying that you are superior to the forces that created Earth itself. You are saying that you are greater than infinity. Outside of that being ludicrous, it puts you in a terribly tenuous position.

The first thing that can happen if you let your ego get between you and your Creator is that He will allow you to try to do everything on your own. This is not a good choice. This means you go back to square one and start over. All that God has given you can disappear in a heartbeat. Including your life.

There's a story about a man who begged God to make Him rich so that he could better serve God's cause on earth. Practically overnight this man became one of the richest men in his country, which happened to be Turkey. He struck it rich in the Cotton Exchange. He was extremely successful beyond his wildest dreams. Then, God sent a messenger to him. It could have been a beggar from the street, we never know. And this messenger asked for money to help with God's work. The messenger reminded the man that the reason he had grown rich was to help with God's work.

The man refused. In fact, he pointed to his cash box and said, "This is my God." Whoa, not a good answer! Within a few weeks the cotton market crashed and our friend lost all that he had. Plus, now he was also deeply in debt.

The man then begged God's forgiveness and promised that he would never again let his ego get out of line. The market once again propelled him to the highest level of prosperity. And once again he denied his debt to God. The story ends with this man, poor as a beggar, walking from town to town, teaching the Universal Laws to anyone who would listen.

All that is required of us to prosper on this planet is two things:

Love and Honor God above all things.

Understand and Follow the Universal Laws.

Do these two things and you will be successful. Avoid doing these two things for any reason and you will have a much, much longer row to hoe.

This is a great system. You follow a few laws and you get to live a great life. I mean, if you receive all your good from God, if He is your protector, your guardian, your provider, your sustainer – who is going to do you harm? Certainly not Mr. Negative. He is no match for the infinite power of the Universe and all that lies above and below it. Not even a contest. Mr. Negative may work harder, but Good is infinitely more powerful.

Once you open your heart to the pulsating power of creation you are free. Your spirit is free from the prison of self. You are free to soar to the farthest reaches of your creativity. You are free to explore your love of life. You are free to search for truth, happiness and everlasting peace. You are free to succeed. Nothing can stop you. Nothing can sway you from the path of Good. Nothing but you and your ego.

Watch the ego. It is our weakest link. Certainly, we need a little ego or we'd be cucumbers. You want more in your life or you wouldn't even be reading this book. We are given the right to choose. We have free will. Used for Good, our free will can propel us to the mountain tops. Used incorrectly, it will pull us down to the lowest level of creation.

There is no "I" in GOD. To find and maintain success with this system you must control the ego. You do not do the work, the Universe does. You ask, God delivers. It is a great system unless you start thinking you are responsible for your own success. I learned that lesson.

Our first full year in business we sold one million dollars in advertising on a technical Web site. In the beginning only a handful of people were even prospects for this site, yet we did well from the very beginning. In 1997 our ad revenue ranked 37th among all websites worldwide. This included all the big corporations pouring millions into their on-line budgets. Quite an accomplishment for a website started out on a card table in a back bedroom. But I wasn't satisfied. I knew we could do more. If we just pushed harder we could do better. I told everybody working for me that I wanted them to work harder, stay later, make more calls. I wanted more research. I wanted more proposals. I wanted higher phone bills. I...I...I...so, guess what happened. I got what I asked for. Expenses went up. Morale went down. We worked longer hours, we wrote more proposals and we made more phone calls. We just did not make nearly as many sales. In fact, we steadily lost business. Finally, we were all exhausted from working too hard. What was I supposed to do?

Nothing. I was supposed to do nothing. I had given God my shopping list and He was delivering. I started thinking I was somehow instrumental in my own success. My ego got in the way and the Universe gave me control of my own destiny. Boy was that a mistake. I did not do nearly as well as I thought I could.

Once I got out of the way and let Creation do the work of creating my success, our sales increased dramatically. We worked a whole lot less and made a whole lot more.

How then can we increase our business, find our true love or get a bigger car? We can't. God does it. He opens the doors. He makes firm the path. He delivers the bounty from His storehouse. And He does it by means over which we have absolutely no control. The Universe will take care of us. By using this system of gaining wealth we accept the fact that we are not in control. God is.

Think of your life as a movie. The script is already written and all you have to do is take each scene one step at a time. But just to keep things interesting the Universe doesn't let you see the script until you've played the scene out. Time and time again you find yourself in seemingly impossible situations which demand trust. You must trust that the Great Spirit directing you will protect you and guide you through even the most difficult scenes. As you play your part in this movie of your life you walk an invisible path. It is an invisible path of trust that leads you to the end you so ultimately desire.

This is how you must live your life. Trust that your path will be made clear. Trust that success is waiting for you. You may not always see where you are going, but you must always step out onto that invisible path, trusting not in yourself, but in God. He guides you. He protects you. He makes you Rich Beyond Your Wildest Dreams.

CHAPTER 27

Ants and the Shower

I need to say a word about consciousness-comprehending the potency of this system of gaining wealth. This is a big concept and not easy to get your arms around. Although the truth of it may be understood by the soul, the mind sometimes takes a little longer to fully grasp the true significance and impact.

On some level, I always believed that God took care of my needs. I had a basic confidence that, no matter what, I would eat, have clothes to wear and have a place to sleep. Moreover, I began to feel that the things that happened to me were predestined. That I met certain people for a reason, that the jobs I had were designed to teach me some specific thing. Most importantly, I felt I would always be led to that which I was meant to do. I felt on some level that the Universe was controlling my life.

I felt this in a general sense only. When it came to the details, I was alone. I always kicked myself for not doing better, for not doing more, for not working harder. I got down on myself all the time, day and night. Of course, once this happened I got exactly what I asked for. More of the same.

Then one day it all came together. I really did not know it back then, but now I do. I know that was the exact starting point of my rise to riches.

I told you in Chapter One that I felt like it all started the day the hawks came to visit me on the beach in sunny California. Actually, as I was writing this book I realized that I made the initial connection much earlier. It is a connection. You have to get it. Something must awaken inside your head and your heart. When it does, everything changes. You truly understand. You become conscious.

I had declared bankruptcy for the second time in ten years and I was very down on myself. My family and I had been evicted from our rented home and we were living in a house where ants used my bathroom as a cemetery. This is the absolute truth. Every morning I was greeted by hundreds of dead ants on the floor of our bathroom. You could sit there and watch these little fellows carry ant carcasses out from under the molding. I had to sweep the floor before I showered. It was not my ideal house. I sprayed. I caulked. It didn't matter. Every morning I was greeted with the bodies of hundreds of dead ants.

Sometimes you have to go down before you can go up. You have to see how bad it can get before you can see your own good. Negativity, like all things in this world, serves a purpose. If you are not accepting your own good, if you are not connecting to the greater truth of the Universe, then you may need to fall so you can rise above the triviality of failure. Truth will out. Eventually you will see the truth, given your willingness to see it. I was not willing to see the truth; that's why I went bankrupt twice in ten years. I didn't get it the first time. I needed another dose of negativity. I had internalized the entire experience as an unforgivable failure on my part. I held on to the emotional burden of those debts long after they were discharged by the federal courts. I blamed myself for the wrong reasons. It's not that I failed to succeed; it's that I was not accepting my own good. I was not letting the Force of Creation guide my life. So I got to do it all over again.

Of course, when you miss the point the first two times, the Universe sends a stronger message the third time. Here I was knee deep in ant carcasses, and once again I was making less money than it took to survive. I simply wasn't making enough money to pay my bills. I was on the same road I'd traveled twice before.

See, what I didn't get was that bankruptcy is a new start. It's a chance to pull yourself out of the guilt and shame of failed ego and step back onto the pathway to God. Remember the Universe intends for all of us to be rich. This life is a gift from the Great Spirit designed to help us grow and expand our consciousness. It is filled with many lessons. And the lesson I had to learn from bankruptcy was to let go. To give up control and allow my success to happen. But since I wasn't getting it, God sent a legion of dead ants to get my attention.

Those dead ants bothered me more than I can explain. I guess they were a physical representation of the dread I was feeling. I was once again on the road to financial disaster and I didn't have the slightest idea what to do about it. I had tried everything. I had sold life insurance because it was, financially speaking, a good business with great residual income. The only trouble was I hated it. I had written advertising, movies and dealer shows. I'd sold carpet, bookkeeping and power factor correction. You name it, I'd done it. My little ad agency was the 39th business or job I'd had since graduating from the University of Nebraska. And I was not even close to making a living, let alone realizing my dreams for success.

Then one night I went ballistic. Through the roof. I

guess I was tired of blaming myself, so I blamed God. How could he make my life so difficult? How could the Universe give me a head full of ideas and then keep me so broke I was unable to do anything about them? Well, I ranted and raved late into the night.

Eventually, although highly agitated, I fell asleep. When I awoke I was in no mood to sweep the ants. I stepped over them and into the shower. I took a long, hot shower that morning. Half awake and half asleep, I really thought more about the ants getting on my feet than my financial woes. I focused on the ants. They seemed like an easier problem.

Finally, I asked myself the big question one more time. How can I get off this road to bankruptcy number three? How can I turn my life around and start making a lot more money? The answer was obvious, I could not do it. I could not turn my life around. I'd already tried everything I knew to do. I was completely out of answers. There was no new business I could start. No new city to move to. My think tank was empty. I simply gave up.

Then it hit me. I got it! Something awakened inside of me. It was a rush of clarity connecting my brain to my heart. It was the essence of understanding. I finally understood what success was all about. If I was going to make more money, God would have to give it to me.

Wow! What a concept. I had dreams of success and no way to realize them. Certainly, if the Power of Creation had given me these dreams, then my dreams were meant to be realized. How would I get all these things I wanted? God was giving them to me. If the Universe could create the Grand Canyon, it could, beyond any doubt, breathe life into my dreams. And since I had big dreams, it meant that I was about to receive a substantial increase in my standard of living.

I was so excited I jumped out of the shower, grabbed a towel and started yelling to my wife. "Diane, wake up. We're rich! We're rich! We're finally rich!"

She, too, was still recovering from the night of yelling and had not had the benefit of my insight. She turned over and looked at me with one eye open while I brushed the dead ants from my feet. It was one of those "he has finally flipped" looks. I quickly explained my deep thoughts. She smiled, pulled her pillow over her head and went back to sleep.

That was it. That was the moment my life changed forever. I cannot explain the change, except that for the first time I saw the specific. I realized that God was taking care of the details. The Universe loved me. Creation wanted me to succeed. Most importantly, God was GIVING me the wealth.

I absolutely knew that I could not change my fate. I knew that I was unable to make even a decent living by my own means. I could not get rich on my own. I had already failed quite miserably, twice. I wanted to be rich, but I was absolutely unable to show even a modicum of success. If I was to be rich, God would have to give it to me. Underline the word give.

God gives us everything.

You do not have to do anything to receive the bounty the Universe has waiting for you. It is already yours. It's waiting for you. Ask and you shall receive. It is that simple. You can have everything you want in life. All you have to do is ask and be willing to receive. God will make you Rich Beyond Your Wildest Dreams.

I'm Rich Beyond My Wildest Dreams

CHAPTER 28

Create the Reality

Have you ever seen a unicorn standing on the edge of a forest as you drive along a mountain road? Have you ever seen a fairy on a late summer evening darting across the front lawn just before dusk? Have you ever seen a mermaid sunning herself on that island just a little too far from shore? No? Why not?

Do you think these things are impossible? Do you find it incomprehensible that these creatures of our imagination could exist? Why? Why is it so hard to believe in fairies and unicorns and mermaids? Are they not logical? Are they outside the boundaries of our concept of reality?

Reality is what we believe it is.

If most of the world believed in fairies, unicorns and mermaids, you would see them running and playing all the time. There are parts of Ireland, today, where saying fairies do not exist could earn you a bloody nose. But because most of the world believes these beautiful creatures are figments of our imagination, they are, for the most part, confined to cartoons, comic books and children's literature. The truth is: Reality does not exist as we know it. Reality exists as we believe it.

Who in this day and age could possibly believe in a

world filled with magical and imaginary creatures? Walt Disney did. He believed the forests were the playground of the wee folk. He believed in talking mice, dogs that drive cars, wealthy ducks and places where little boys never grow up. Walt Disney believed so strongly in this world that now little children all over the world believe it, too. Go to Mickey's house in Toon Town and watch the faces of the little kids that have their pictures taken with Mickey Mouse. They believe.

We tend to believe that which we already accept. Trends tend to continue. This makes it very difficult for us to realize the vastness of our creation. It limits us. It denies us the opportunity to grow and evolve.

For example, many people believe that since there has always been war, there must always be war. That somehow it is intrinsic to human nature to want to kill each other. That somehow it is part of our makeup to hate and destroy. Hogwash! This is exactly the opposite of our nature. Human beings of all colors and backgrounds want precisely the same things. Peace. Love. Unity. Joy. Happiness. Wealth and well-being.

It is our perception of reality that keeps us from having these things. It is our limited concept of what is real that stands between us and Universal Peace. Many people still believe that anyone who is not like them, like their immediate reality, is bad. They call these other people names. They disparage their culture and their traditions. Why? Because they have not yet come to understand that this world is filled with many realities. Whatever names you call other people are only an expression of your lack, your lack of visualizing a greater, more powerful truth, your lack of understanding the fundamental building block of a better reality. You are only talking about yourself. You are denying yourself the power to create a reality which is incredibly Rich Beyond Your Wildest Dreams.

Who says there are no fairies? Who says unicorns are figments of our imagination? What is an imagination? Where do these unreal images come from in the first place? How can we possibly imagine something that does not exist? Don't we get everything from God? Don't we get our imagination from God? Would God, who is all Good, allow us to imagine that which is not true?

If every thought is a command, who determines which reality we create? Two centuries ago doctors said fever was best treated with leeches. Is that your reality? Less than one century ago people said that God never meant for humans to fly. Is that your reality? The Wright brothers did not agree and now we all believe in airplanes. Who determines your reality? You do, of course. You have the right to believe whatever you want to believe. And whatever you believe is true. You have the power of your thoughts. You can create any reality you choose.

Well, then, what about the unicorn? Does she exist? Airplanes, trains and automobiles did not always exist. Somebody had to believe in them. Somebody somewhere imagined that computers, televisions, radios, toasters, liquid non-allergenic soap, cable cars and diet soda existed. Not to mention the billions of other things that make up our present reality. What about the other things our minds can imagine, but are not yet accepted as real? Starships? Food replicators? Active, healthy life spans of 150 years? Instantaneous travel? Intelligent life on other planets? Unicorns? Fairies? World Peace? Love and harmony among all humankind?

If you can think it, you can have it. You create your own reality. You are not limited by the reality your parents created. You are not limited by the reality your grandparents created. You have the power to create a kinder, more loving world in which to live. We cannot afford another world war. Albert Einstein once said, "I don't know what weapons they will use to fight WW III, but I know the weapons they use for WW IV will be sticks and stones." Actually, it is worse than that. Unless we consciously choose a more loving, tolerant reality we may not have another choice at all.

We have entered a powerful new age. It is an age of cooperation. It is an age where good wins and every creature counts. For the first time, the people of the world have the opportunity to create their own future. The Internet allows us to talk to one another across all boundaries. We can decide for ourselves what is true and what is false. We can decide which reality we choose to live. This is the opportunity that billions have given their lives for. All those who have ever lived on this planet have helped bring us from the age of mammoth hunting to this, the age of Maturity. A time when humankind recognizes the Good within each and every one.

It is time for us to step forward. It is time for the good to win. It is time for us to throw down the sharp toys of our childhood and accept the mantle of leadership. It is time for us to gather our forces for the opening of a new century, a new millenium and a new age. It is time to step out of the clouds of fear and misunderstanding. It is time for us to take our place at the front of the line. It is time to eschew doubt and hatred. It is time to create a new Reality.

The Reality that we create will determine the course of the world for the next 500,000 years and more. Expand your thinking. As John F. Kennedy said, "Some look at a mountain and ask why. I ask why not?"

We can create any reality we choose. We can forgive the pain and injustice of the past. We can change the destiny of all the lives that have gone before us. We can release our anger and our hatred. We can leave behind the empty promises of the ego. We can accept and magnify the love that emanates from every atom in creation. We can turn to the Goodness of the Universe to provide for our prosperity. We can choose a new way. A new brighter path.

Why not choose a rich, bounteous future? Why not choose a future filled with all the good things your heart desires? Success? Love? Happiness? Wealth? Joy? We can each and every one have everything we want in life? It's yours for the asking. The Universe has given you the power. All you have to do is ask. Ask and you Create the Reality.

Imagine what you want your world to be like. Keep in mind that you can have any good that you can imagine. That everyone loves everyone else. This is easy to do. Give up hate and only love remains. No one can threaten you, because the Universe protects you. It is the source of all your good. You are dependent upon no one else.

Step out on that ledge that you cannot see. The ledge that leads you to happiness, joy and prosperity forever. Never worry again. Never for one instant doubt that Creation is taking care of you. Never doubt that the Universe loves and encourages your goodness and forgives your mistakes. Reach out. Take that step. You are one step away from a prosperity you can barely imagine, a reality of which you may have only dreamed.

Open the door to your mansion. Visualize the impossible dream. Surround yourself with the riches of a king. They are yours not for the taking, but for the asking. "Ask and ye shall receive. Seek and ye shall find. Knock

and the door shall be opened." And you shall be Rich
Beyond Your Wildest Dreams.

CHAPTER 29

The Song of Success

We have come to the end of our time together for now. I find it a little sad. I have enjoyed sharing this with you more than I can easily express. I hope you get as much from reading it as we did writing it. As I said before, my daughter, Penelope, was instrumental in this creation. I must add that my wife, Diane, not only made it possible for us to write, but corrected my thousand and one mistakes, as she has throughout our life together.

Read the book again, please. Some of these concepts take a while to digest and hold as your own. Take what you can or will. Leave what you do not want behind. This is for you. Not me. I am already Rich Beyond My Wildest Dreams. I am. I am. I am.

I have one more suggestion for you. This is a treat, really. I learned it while writing this book. At one point I was feeling low. My income was down and I was having a hard time seeing my dreams come true. I was not really convinced that I was Rich Beyond My Wildest Dreams. Marilyn showed me how to convince myself. I want to share that with you now.

The title of this book is really a song. Which I intimated earlier. Now, you get to sing this song. For one week and only one week sing, "I'm Rich Beyond My Wildest Dreams. I am. I am. I am." You'll have to find your own tune. I started with the Battle Hymn of the Republic, but you may find that a bit slow. I sang this song for seven days and then I stopped. It was hard to stop. I wanted to continue, but there is power in doing it only seven days. So I stopped. In the next seven days we sold more advertising than we had ever sold in one week. In fact, we sold twice as much advertising in those next seven days as we had in the whole previous month.

The secret is you can only sing this song for one week, seven days, then you must stop. So, sing it at every opportunity. Sing while you are in the car, in the back yard, alone watching TV or playing with the dog. Sing it often, because you will not want to stop either once those seven days are up.

There are other songs you can sing for a week. Songs like "I am slim and trim and healthy. I am. I am. I am." Of course, you should only do one song in a week.

The "I am" is an affirmation. You are calling out to God to work through you.

Oh, if you need to contact us, our email address is listed on the back of the first title page along with our physical address and Web site address. Come to our Web site or use the email for questions or help. I cannot guarantee I will able to respond to questions sent to our physical address.

Well, good luck. See you in Saint Moritz.

The band is still playing. And it's your turn to take the stage. You have the skills. You know the secrets. Everything you want in life is now yours for the asking.

I'm Rich Beyond
My Wildest Dreams.
I am. I am. Iam.

I'm Rich Beyond
My Wildest Dreams.
I am. I am. I am.

I'm Rich Beyond
My Wildest Dreams
I am. I am. I am.

I am. I am. I am.
I am. I am. I am.

I'm Rich Beyond My Wildest Dreams

"Share this powerful new book with a friend"

I'm Rich Beyond My Wildest Dreams.

"I am. I am. I am."

How to Get Everything You Want in Life.

by Thomas L. Pauley and Penelope J. Pauley

Please ship _____ copies of this book to:

Name_____

Street Address_____

City _____ State _____ Zip_____

E-mail address _____

Send check or money order for $24.95 per book (includes shipping) to:
RichDreams Publishing
4023 Birch Street, Ste A, PMB 271
Newport Beach, CA 92660-2231

Visit our Web site at **http://www.richdreams.com**

"Share this powerful new book with a friend"

I'm Rich Beyond My Wildest Dreams.

"I am. I am. I am."

How to Get Everything You Want in Life.

by Thomas L. Pauley and Penelope J. Pauley

Please ship _____ copies of this book to:

Name_____

Street Address_____

City _____ State _____ Zip_____

E-mail address _____

Send check or money order for $24.95 per book (includes shipping) to:
RichDreams Publishing
4023 Birch Street, Ste A, PMB 271
Newport Beach, CA 92660-2231

Visit our Web site at **http://www.richdreams.com**